Cambridge Eler

Elements in Religion and Mo
edited by
Paul K. Moser
Loyola University Chicago
Chad Meister
*Affiliate Scholar, Ansari Institute for Global Engagement with Religion,
University of Notre Dame*

MONOTHEISM
AND FUNDAMENTALISM

Prevalence, Potential, and Resilience

Rik Peels
Vrije Universiteit Amsterdam

CAMBRIDGE
UNIVERSITY PRESS

Shaftesbury Road, Cambridge CB2 8EA, United Kingdom

One Liberty Plaza, 20th Floor, New York, NY 10006, USA

477 Williamstown Road, Port Melbourne, VIC 3207, Australia

314–321, 3rd Floor, Plot 3, Splendor Forum, Jasola District Centre,
New Delhi – 110025, India

103 Penang Road, #05-06/07, Visioncrest Commercial, Singapore 238467

Cambridge University Press is part of Cambridge University Press & Assessment,
a department of the University of Cambridge.

We share the University's mission to contribute to society through the pursuit of
education, learning and research at the highest international levels of excellence.

www.cambridge.org
Information on this title: www.cambridge.org/9781009500487

DOI: 10.1017/9781009309653

First published 2024

A catalogue record for this publication is available from the British Library.

ISBN 978-1-009-50048-7 Hardback
ISBN 978-1-009-30964-6 Paperback
ISSN 2631-3014 (online)
ISSN 2631-3006 (print)

Cambridge University Press & Assessment has no responsibility for the persistence
or accuracy of URLs for external or third-party internet websites referred to in this
publication and does not guarantee that any content on such websites is, or will
remain, accurate or appropriate.

Monotheism and Fundamentalism

Prevalence, Potential, and Resilience

Elements in Religion and Monotheism

DOI: 10.1017/9781009309653
First published online: April 2024

Rik Peels
Vrije Universiteit Amsterdam
Author for correspondence: Rik Peels, h.d.peels@vu.nl

Abstract: This Element explores the relation between monotheism and fundamentalism. It does so from both an empirical perspective and a more theoretical one that combines theological and philosophical insights. The empirical part addresses how, as a matter of fact, particularly quantitively, monotheism and fundamentalism relate to one another. The more theoretical part studies the relation between the two by considering the doctrine of God and the issue of exclusion, theories of revelation, and ethics. Finally, the Element considers whether monotheism has particular resources that can be employed in mitigating the consequences of or even altogether preventing fundamentalism. This title is also available as Open Access on Cambridge Core.

Keywords: monotheism, fundamentalism, resilience, violence, exclusivism

ISBNs: 9781009500487 (HB), 9781009309646 (PB), 9781009309653 (OC)
ISSNs: 2631-3014 (online), 2631-3006 (print)

Contents

Introduction

The Question

The core question that this Element addresses is how monotheism relates to fundamentalism. A straightforward suggestion often voiced not only in public debate but also in the academic literature is that monotheism causes or at least raises the likelihood of fundamentalism.[1] Monotheism, after all, claims that there is only one God and that only that one true God ought to be worshiped. One might think that this belief or associated doctrines and practices easily lead to intolerance toward others, particularly those who are not of the specific monotheistic brand that one belongs to oneself.[2] An example from the public debate is Jean-Pierre Lehmann (2006) in *The Globalist*:

> If you have only one god, and you believe that god is all powerful and omniscient, and you come across someone who does not agree, then you may feel it is your duty to kill him. If, on the other hand, you believe there are hundreds, indeed thousands of gods, and that none can be totally almighty or omniscient, then you are likely to be far more tolerant. The great pre-Christian civilizations of Greece and Rome had no religious wars and had a far healthier view of their frolicking gods and goddesses than the intolerant monotheistic Christianity that later came to dominate Europe.

Since our primary focus in this Element will be on the academic literature, let us consider a few quotes from leading scholars in religious studies, law, and sociology. Steve Bruce (2008, 99–100), for instance, notes that

> while any shared religious identity can become the focus for political mobilization, the greater the existing cohesion (which we can see, for example, in the ease of talking about orthodoxy and heresy) the more likely it is that adherents will produce a fundamentalist response to modernization. In that sense the monotheistic religions of Judaism, Christianity and Islam offer much more fertile soil for fundamentalism than Hinduism and Buddhism. Because there is one God, whose nature and will is revealed in sacred sources, clear lines can be drawn between believers and unbelievers.

---

[1] As Buijs (2013) rightly points out, it is not always clear what exactly the claim amounts to. When it comes to monotheism and violence in particular, for instance, is the claim that monotheism *causes* violence, *statistically correlates with* violence, *theologically justifies the use of* violence, or yet something else?

[2] This objection to monotheism can be found in the writings of several influential philosophers who are known for being critical of religion; for example, David Hume in his 1757 work *Natural History of Religion*, Arthur Schopenhauer in *Parerga and Paralipomena* (published in 1851), and arguably also William James in his 1990 book *A Pluralistic Universe*.

Others do not use the term *fundamentalism* but relate monotheism to phenomena that are often associated with fundamentalism, such as violence.[3] An example is Jan Assmann (2005, 141–2):

> Monotheism required a firm decision and correspondingly strong concepts about "the other," for which a whole new vocabulary was created: the "heathens," "pagans," "gentiles," "unbelievers," "idolaters," "heretics" etc. The strength of the decision and the firmness of the conviction imply an element of violence. . . . It is impossible to deny that—at least potentially— this kind of religion implies a new type of violence, religiously motivated and directed against those who, in the light of that new distinction, appear to be the enemies of god. . . . Violence belongs to what could be called the "core-semantics" of monotheism.[4]

Regina Schwartz extends the list of monotheism's ramifications by mentioning not merely violence but also exclusivism, patriarchy, misogyny, authoritarianism, othering, and particularism. She speaks of "the myth of monotheism" and argues that it is "a system in which identity depends upon rejection of the Other and subjection of the Self" (Schwartz 1997, 31). She claims that there are two principles in the Bible: the principle of metaphysical scarcity, on the one hand, which leads to conflict over limited resources, and the principle of plenitude or generosity, on the other. Unfortunately, she argues, in the Bible the former trumps the latter, and monotheism is its embodiment:

> Scarcity is encoded in the Bible as a principle of Oneness (one land, one people, one nation) and in monotheistic thinking (one Deity), it becomes a demand of exclusive allegiance that threatens with the violence of exclusion. When that thinking is translated into secular formations about peoples, "one nation under God" becomes less comforting than threatening. (Schwartz 1997, xi)

Monotheism forges a collective identity by negation: one is a people set apart or even over against the other, whereas polytheism endorses toleration and even appreciation of difference.[5]

Various scholars do not confine themselves to Judaism or Christianity but make such claims about monotheisms in general. According to Rodney Stark, for instance, particularly in his influential twin monographs *One True God: Historical Consequences of Monotheism* (2001) and *For the Glory of God: How Monotheism Led to Reformations, Science, Witch-Hunts, and the End of Slavery* (2003), there is a certain inherent logic to any kind of monotheism: it entails that

---

[3] As Meral (2018, 1–26) argues, this particularly holds for Islam.

[4] Equally critical of the Abrahamic religions, but also of various secular systems, such as atheistic communism and fascism, and equally admiring of Egypt as Assmann is Sloterdijk (2007).

[5] See Schwartz (1997, 30–3, 76, 119). In a couple of places, she relates the issue to fundamentalism; see Schwartz (1997, 122, 153).

the one God one believes in is better than the other gods—he trumps them. Inevitably, this will lead to schism and conflict, even though Stark is quick to add that it has also led to the birth of science and, in the long run, the abolition of slavery (see Stark 2001, 2003).

Others go even further, possibly influenced by the horrendous events of 9/11. They believe monotheism is not just conducive to fundamentalism but increases the risk of religious terrorism. Paul Cliteur, for instance, argues that there are several elements in the monotheistic Abrahamic religions that terrorists use to justify their actions and that their interpretations are not arbitrary but have to do with what these religions stand for. Discussing various passages in the First Testament,[6] such as God ordering the Israelites to kill the Amalekites, the story of Jephthah, and the allegedly divine command for Abraham to kill his son Isaak, Cliteur says:

> These are at the very least "dangerous" stories. By that I mean that religious terrorists can easily find inspiration in them. . . . Monotheistic religions provide starting points for radicals to put the country's law and morality aside and to orient themselves toward a high transcendent religious law and morality.[7]

He then argues that we should abandon monotheism and adopt what he calls "cultural polytheism." This differs from theological polytheism in that it does not actually take it that there are different gods but merely that belief in different gods who share power and hold each other accountable, such as the polytheistic faith of the Romans and the Greeks, is a good thing.

Quite a few authors, then, both in the public debate and in the academic literature, make statements to the effect that there is an empirical or even theological connection between monotheism, on the one hand, and fundamentalism and related phenomena, such as violence, on the other.[8] However, many others adopt a different approach. For example, in explaining early twentieth-century American evangelical fundamentalism—as we shall see, the prototype of fundamentalism—George Marsden, probably the leading scholar in the study of Christian fundamentalism, appeals to a wide variety of macrofactors. Among them are (1) urbanization together with migration of new groups with more liberal public ethics, such as

---

[6] In this Element, I will consistently speak of First and Second Testaments rather than Old and New Testaments since *Old* may sound pejorative to some or may wrongly suggest that it has passed only to be replaced by the New.

[7] See Cliteur (2010, 172, 194). The translation here from Dutch is my own.

[8] One may be tempted to explain this negative portrayal of monotheism and, in some cases, religion more generally by appeal to a secular bias among contemporary Western academics. For what that secular bias would amount to, see Dawson (2018). Here, I will sidestep the issue of what the proper explanation of these criticisms is—even though I lean in the direction suggested—and address these scholars' portrayal of the relation between monotheism and fundamentalism head-on.

Catholics, Jews, and Freemasons; (2) violent sentiments evoked by strong war rhetoric during World War I; and (3) the increasing influence of liberal scholarship, historical-biblical criticism in particular, and the impact of Darwinian evolutionary theory (see Marsden 1980, 9–61). Nowhere does Marsden appeal to anything having to do with the beliefs and practices of monotheism in general or even those of Christianity in particular. In fact, the majority of fundamentalism scholars seems to assume there is no such connection between monotheism and fundamentalism. Who, then, is right?

This Element explores the relation between monotheism and fundamentalism. Yet, it is not narrowly confined to the issue of whether, as the quotes just given suggest, monotheism is conducive to fundamentalism. Of course, that is an important question, and it is dealt with extensively in Section 2. However, there are further critically important questions to be asked. For instance, is there anything about monotheisms—in terms of their beliefs, doctrines, ideas, and theologies—that steers believers in the direction of fundamentalism? This is an important question, regardless of whether, as an empirical matter of fact, there is more fundamentalism in monotheisms than in other religions and worldviews. Another important question asks whether monotheisms may provide certain resources to fight or mitigate the harmful side of fundamentalism or to create resilience against it. In exploring the relation between monotheism and fundamentalism, then, we will go far beyond the unduly narrow issue of whether there is more fundamentalism in monotheism than in nonmonotheistic religions and secular worldviews.

The relation between monotheism and fundamentalism can be explored from at least three different perspectives. From an *empirical* point of view, one can ask whether as a matter of fact fundamentalism is more prevalent in monotheism than in polytheistic religions, animistic religions, and secular movements. This will be the focus of Section 2. From a more *theoretical* perspective— here, a philosophical and theological one—we can ask whether there are certain doctrines, concepts, ideas, or theories in the theologies of monotheism that steer believers in the direction of fundamentalism. This will be addressed in Section 3. Finally, one can adopt a more *normative* perspective by asking whether monotheism has resources that are useful in fighting or mitigating harmful consequences of fundamentalism or that may even prevent it altogether. This will be addressed in Section 4.

What Is Monotheism?

Let us start with a few preliminary words on the crucial term *monotheism* (the term *fundamentalism* will be discussed in Section 1). The word *monotheism* derives from the combination of the Greek *monos* (single) and *theos* (god).

Monotheism can be defined as the idea that there is only one god or deity, referred to as "God" and usually understood as an all-supreme or perfect being. It is preferable to speak of "idea" rather than "belief," because this idea can be embodied not only in the religious believers' beliefs and other propositional attitudes (like hopes and desires) but also in their doctrines, practices, rituals, and symbols. Monotheism comes in two guises: exclusive or prophetic monotheism says that there is only one God, whereas inclusive or pluriform monotheism says that there are multiple gods or godly forms, but that they are all extensions of the same God. Virtually all varieties of monotheism ascribe further properties to God, such as that he[9] is transcendent, personal, distinct from the world, and superior to the world, but these are usually not thought of as essential to monotheism (thus also Leitane 2013, 1355).

Monotheism thus defined is found in the Abrahamic religions: Judaism, Christianity, Islam, Mandaeanism, the Bahá'í faith, and Rastafarianism. But it is also found in other, non-Abrahamic religions: Bábism, Cheondoism, Druzism, Eckankar, Sikhism, such traditions within Hinduism as Shaivism and Vaishnavism, Seicho-no-le, Tenrikyo, Yazidism (closely related to Islam and particularly Sufism), and Zoroastrianism. Early monotheistic elements can be found in Atenism and Yahwism. Finally, it can be found in theo-philosophical traditions like deism, which says that faith in God is a natural religion that does not require divine revelation and that God created the world but is no longer directly involved in it. There are also boundary cases of monotheism, such as Vedantic monism in India and the philosophies of Xenophon and other pre-Socratics. These are sometimes referred to as pseudomonotheisms.

Three notions that are closely related to monotheism are henotheism, monolatrism, and summodeism. *Henotheism* can be defined as the idea that the believer should worship one God, whether or not other gods exist.[10] Monolatrism can be understood as the view that there are other gods, but only the one true God is to be worshiped (the latter is also called relative, potential, or insular monotheism). And summodeism can be summarized as the worship of a supreme deity who is the head of a pantheon of other deities that exist as

---

[9] In this Element, I will consistently refer to God with the pronouns *he* and *him*, even though God, on the majority view in most monotheisms, is neither male nor female (as God is not a human being). The two main alternatives face some serious problems for the purposes of this study: plural pronouns (they/them/theirs) would not fit well with what monotheism stands for, and feminine pronouns (she/her) would conflict with what most fundamentalisms believe about God.

[10] *Henotheism* is sometimes also defined as situational monotheism—that is, as worshiping one deity in a specific situation, like prayer or sacrifice, as if that god had all the functions of the other gods.

aspects, functions, or manifestations of this high god.[11] It is common in monotheism, henotheism, monolatrism, and summodeism to think of God as the high god or the Supreme Being. A final, closely related phenomenon is so-called *ethical monotheism*. This term was invented by Abraham Kuenen in 1877 and used by such theologians and philosophers as Julius Wellhausen and Hermann Cohen. The core idea is that only God is righteous among the gods and that he demands responsible behavior from humans.

In this Element, we shall zoom in on Abrahamic monotheisms, as the term *fundamentalism* is most clearly applicable to certain movements within these religions. In fact, for the sake of focus and clarity, we shall largely confine ourselves to what are arguably the three most influential varieties of Abrahamic monotheism: Christianity, Judaism, and Islam.

Relevance

Exactly why does it matter precisely how monotheism and fundamentalism are related to one another? There are at least three theoretical payoffs and one practical potential benefit to an exploration of this issue. As to the theoretical payoffs: Understanding the exact relation between monotheism and fundamentalism might shed light on how we can understand, explain, and perhaps even predict fundamentalism or its absence. It may contribute to the debate on whether we should employ the notion of fundamentalism at all—whether, for instance, there is enough similarity across different monotheisms to speak of fundamentalism in each case. And it may also provide a deeper understanding of why particular properties, such as literalism and infallibilism, are more salient in some fundamentalist movements, while others, such as hostility toward the out-group or moral dualism, are more salient in other fundamentalist movements. As to the practical payoffs, monotheism might have particular resources that could be employed for fighting fundamentalism or mitigating its consequences and thus contribute to processes of cognitive and behavioral deradicalization, as well as for building resilience against it.

This Element seeks to depolarize a debate that is often heated and abounds with sweeping statements. It does so in a radically interdisciplinary way: it provides sober inspection of what we know on the basis of *empirical work*, it *philosophically* explores whether the beliefs and practices of monotheisms are conducive to fundamentalism, and it *theologically* studies the resilience potential of various monotheistic traditions.

---

[11] The distinction between henotheism and monolatrism is admittedly somewhat stipulative, but I believe it works well for our purposes in this Element.

The main question of this Element is, perhaps, abnormally large: How does monotheism relate to fundamentalism? Entire books have been written about specific monotheistic fundamentalist movements in specific countries in a specific time. Yet it is important every now and then to take a step back, adopt a bird's-eye perspective, and ask a really big question. We shall see that doing so gives us unique and valuable insights.

1 What Is Fundamentalism?

1.1 Introduction

Let me be up-front about the fact that *fundamentalism* is a contested term, possibly even an essentially contested one, both when it comes to its accuracy and when it comes to its fecundity. Among its proponents are the leaders of the seminal *Fundamentalism Project*, Martin Marty and R. Scott Appleby (1991–5; see also Almond, Appleby, and Sivan 2003), but also Malise Ruthven (2004), Bruce Lawrence (1989), and—particularly influential among the larger public—Karen Armstrong (2000). Those who are hesitant about using the term point to its ambiguity and argue that it mistakenly lumps together phenomena that have little or even nothing in common, that it is Western centered, that the notion is too strongly tied to Christian tropes, that it is plain offensive or hostile in that it labels people with views that are thought to be disagreeable, extreme, or irrational, that it diminishes the legitimacy of religious paradigms, that it polarizes the debate on the public functions of religions, or that in using the term, one distances and delegitimates the other.[12] According to Jean Axelrad Cahan (2014, 109), for instance, "the term is too burdened by ideational and political biases to be a sound scholarly tool." And Khalid Yahya Blankinship (2014, 158) summarizes his criticisms by saying it is "a term of abuse." Equally critical of the notion are Jay M. Harris, Susan Harding, Simon A. Wood, Daniel Varisco, and Gabriele Marranci.[13] They usually suggest that everything that has happened over the last few decades can be equally well or even better captured by such terms as *nationalism, traditionalism, conservatism, orthodoxy, maximalism, communalism, populism, separatism, sectarianism,* and *exclusivism.* Also, what used to be described as *Islamic fundamentalism,* they say, is better dubbed *Islamism* or *political Islam.*

---

[12] For these criticisms, see Blankinship (2014, 146); Pohl (2014, 228).

[13] See various voices in Wood and Watt (2014), particularly those of Simon A. Wood and Khalid Yahya Blankinship, and Harding (1991, 2000); Harris (1994); Varisco (2007); Marranci (2009); Wood (2011). Wood and Watt are critical of using *fundamentalism* beyond Christianity, more critical of using it beyond the Abrahamic religions, and presumably even more critical of using it beyond religion (in fact, its alleged implausibility may explain why they do not even mention that as an option).

This Element will use the term *fundamentalism*, not merely because the series editors extended an invitation to write an Element on monotheism and fundamentalism but also for a pragmatic and an epistemic reason. The pragmatic one is that the term, despite the many challenges that have been leveled against it, is firmly entrenched both in public and in academic debates. As Gordon Newby (2014, 251) rightly notes:

> For those authors who advocate abolishing the use of the term, it is, in my opinion, too late. Not only is it in general used across the various registers of English; the Library of Congress has also designated a special classification for books on the subject. As many have done, it is possible to invoke the term and then explain how the term has been used and will then be used by the author. Then the term can be used or avoided, but educating, thereby, the reader to the possibilities and limitations of the term, strengthening the author's own argument about the material under investigation.

I have no doubt that after decades of use and thousands of publications, the term will not go away. In that regard, it differs from terms like *Mohammedanism* or *primitive religion*, which show a steep decline in use ever since they were rightly criticized. Rather than trying to discard a notion that will be used anyway, we should seek to remove as much ambiguity about it as possible.

The epistemic reason for sticking to the word *fundamentalism* is that, as we shall see, using the term is fruitful in that it shows crucial similarities across Abrahamic, non-Abrahamic religious, and even secular varieties of fundamentalism. Let me give just two examples. First, Christian, Muslim, and Hindu fundamentalisms first surfaced in the 1920s,[14] and arguably the same holds for fascism and Jewish fundamentalism. This is because they are all responses to particularly modern developments that took flight in the early twentieth century, developments related to globalization, new ideas in science, and new approaches in ethics. Second, numerous scholars have argued there is something like a fundamentalist mindset that can be found across many radically different religious and secular movements.[15] This squares well with the analysis of fundamentalism that I propose, which will be one in terms of stereotypical properties. That it acknowledges similarities between different fundamentalist movements is one of the things that make it empirically fruitful. Of course, this should not induce us to overlook crucial differences—in fact, at various junctures this Element will elaborate on them. In fact, we shall see that my analysis of fundamentalism in terms of stereotypical properties—rather than necessary and sufficient conditions—can do justice to the radical differences between fundamentalisms worldwide.

---

[14] As Clarke (2017, 65) also notes.   [15] See, for instance, the essays in Strozier et al. (2010).

1.2 The History of a Concept

Tracing the origin of the concept of fundamentalism requires going back to early twentieth-century America. The term was first used by Baptist journalist Curtis Lee Laws to denote a movement that he thought was present at the North Baptist Convention in Buffalo, New York, in 1920. The term was derived from what conservative evangelicals called "the fundamentals." They had formulated these principles to make explicit what they believed to be their faith's non-negotiables, things such as Christ's virgin birth, his subsidiary atonement on the cross, his physical resurrection, his imminent return and eschatological thousand-year reign of peace, the inerrancy of the First and Second Testaments, and the Trinity of God. Many of these alleged fundamentals can be found in more detail in the collection of booklets *The Fundamentals: A Testimony to the Truth*, published between 1910 and 1915 and edited by A. C. Dixon, Louis Meyer, and Reuben Torrey (see Torrey 1917). These fundamentals were formulated because of what conservative evangelicals considered harmful and dangerous modern developments, such as the rise of evolutionary theory, historical-biblical criticism, liberal systematic theology, and liberal ethics.

Early Christian fundamentalists can be characterized as follows. First, they were often well organized. For instance, 6,000 people took part in the 1919 World Christian Fundamentals Associations (WCFA) meeting. Moreover, contrary to the stereotypical portrayal of fundamentalists, Christian fundamentalists could be found not only in the southern parts but all over the United States, and many of them lived in the larger cities. Christian fundamentalism was significantly more popular among White Americans than among Black or other colored Americans, though. Its leaders were all males, but women did a lot of behind-the-scenes work and in fact, maybe somewhat surprisingly, the majority of the fundamentalist movement was female. Christian fundamentalism at the outset was a middle-class movement (see Watt 2014, 23–4).

This early twentieth-century movement among conservative evangelical and Baptist Christians in the United States and a couple of places in the United Kingdom is nowadays often referred to as *historical fundamentalism*. It is to be contrasted with *global fundamentalism*, which denotes fundamentalism across many different kinds of religions. Use of the latter is more recent. Since the Islamic revival in the 1970s and particularly the Iranian revolution in 1979 with Ayatollah Khomeini as the leading figure, groups of scholars have been using the term *fundamentalism* to also denote Islamic fundamentalism, nowadays including Wahhabism, jihadism, and the Muslim Brotherhood. In fact, *fundamentalism* often now primarily refers to Islamic fundamentalism. Soon after this development in the 1970s, the term was also employed to refer to fundamentalisms in other Abrahamic religions, such as the Kach and Haredi movements in Judaism. Furthermore, others used *fundamentalism* for what they thought of as fundamentalist movements in non-Abrahamic religions, such as the Rashtriya Swayamsevak Sangh (RSS) in Hinduism and varieties of nationalist Sinhala Buddhism. *The Fundamentalism Project* (Marty and Appleby 1991–5), which provided a state-of-the-art overview of empirical work on fundamentalism, is a prime example of this broader use of the term.

In fact, in the last few decades, the term has even been employed to refer to nonreligious movements. Among the secular movements sometimes characterized as fundamentalist are neo-Nazism and fascism more generally (West 2016), ecofundamentalism (Hannesson 2014), communism (Wnuk-Lipiński 2004, 281–4), feminist fundamentalism, market or capitalist fundamentalism, and scientific imperialism or scientistic fundamentalism (see Peels 2023b). Others have rejected the inclusion of secular movements and confined fundamentalism to religious phenomena (e.g., Armstrong 2000; Bruce 2008). All this clearly raises the question of what the proper limits of the term are, if any principled limits can be formulated at all.

1.3 Fundamentalism as a Family Resemblance Concept

In the literature, we find definitions of fundamentalism in terms of necessary and sufficient conditions, such as the one provided by Luca Ozzano (2017, 133), who defines a *fundamentalist movement* as

> a more or less coherent array of groups and organizations which, grounding its ideology on a selective re-interpretation of sacred texts, acts in the public sphere in order to make as suitable as possible to its worldview lifestyles, laws and institutions, taking a dialectic stance towards modernity and opposing other segments of society, identified as unyielding rivals.

The problem, however, is that the movements often considered to be fundamentalist seem simply too diverse for a truly rich analysis in terms of necessary and sufficient conditions. Hindu ethnonationalism, for instance, shares only a few properties with Christian and Islamist fundamentalism. This holds a fortiori if we seek to include secular varieties of fundamentalism, particularly because some of them are, in a sense, complete opposites, such as left-wing ecofundamentalism on the one hand and market fundamentalism on the other.

Various authors have suggested that fundamentalism is, therefore, better understood as a *family resemblance concept* (e.g., Almond, Appleby, and Sivan 2003, 90–115; Almond, Sivan, and Appleby 1995; Droogers 2005; Marty and Appleby 1991; Pfürtner 1997). The idea of a family resemblance was first formulated by Ludwig Wittgenstein in his *Philosophical Investigations*

(1953, Sections 66–9). He noted that some things seem to be related to one another not by way of sharing certain necessary and sufficient conditions but by way of belonging to a family whose members share some properties, but not others, with one another. He called this a family likeness, or *Familienähnlichkeit*. The prime example that he used was that of a game: some games are regulated by rules, others are not; some games are for fun, others are not; some games are group activities, others are not. The only way to make sense of what makes something a game, he suggested, is to formulate a list of stereotypical properties of games: the more of these properties something has, the stronger a candidate it is for being a game. This means there are paradigm examples of games, ones that have virtually all of those stereotypical properties, such as a public soccer match, and boundary cases, which have relatively few, such as a person repeatedly throwing a ball against a wall out of boredom.

It is, of course, to some extent controversial exactly what those stereotypical properties of fundamentalism are. Elsewhere, I have defended a particular account of fundamentalism called the BicFam account. I employed this portmanteau because the account combines a biconditional analysis (Bic) in terms of rather general properties that are necessary and sufficient conditions with an analysis in terms of family resemblance (Fam) and implies that fundamentalism is a *big family* of quite different kinds of movements. With regard to what they stand for—their content—we can distinguish three types of properties of fundamentalisms: they are reactionary, they are modern, and they embrace a particular kind of narrative.[16] Let me explain what I mean by each of these.

1.4 The Stereotypical Properties of Fundamentalism

The first type of properties concerns the fact that fundamentalist movements are reactionary or—a slightly less pejorative term—responsive to modern or modernist developments.[17] Some scholars in the field, such as Martin Marty and Scott Appleby, even consider this to be the defining characteristic of fundamentalism. This means that they are not freestanding movements, but that they are primarily a critical response to what they consider to be deficient or even threatening modern developments. They set their agenda in response to them (see Almond, Appleby, and Sivan 2003; Battaglia 2017; Heywood 2012, Chapter 10). What such modernity amounts to differs from case to case. We

---

[16] This overview of properties is based on Peels (2022).

[17] In this Element, I will use the terms *modernity* and *modernism*, as well as *modern* and *modernist*, as equivalents. One could, of course, make a distinction among them—for instance, by making *modernity* denote a time period and *modernism* the philosophy and values propagated by the majority in that time period.

already saw that early twentieth-century evangelicals responded to liberal ethics, historical-biblical criticism, and evolutionary theory. Other modern developments that came in the wake of the Enlightenment were secularity, relativism, globalization, growing religious diversity, abandonment of trad-itional religious models and values, and the heritage of colonialism.

Fundamentalist movements not only reject these modern developments but also offer alternatives. Instead of liberal ethics, they propagate traditional gender roles, are pro-lifers, and sometimes acknowledge fewer rights for women, homosexuals, and people of other faiths and ethnicities. Hindu funda-mentalists, for instance, do not acknowledge the same rights for Muslims as they do for Hindus. Fundamentalist Calvinists reject ordination of women as deacons, elders, or pastors. In rejecting science, such as evolutionary theory, bioethics, and big bang cosmology, they appeal to scripture as a reliable or even infallible source of knowledge. Sometimes, they provide rival, allegedly scien-tific approaches, such as that of creationism—witness such phenomena as the Institute for Creation Research and the *Journal of Creation*.[18]

Things are more complicated for left-wing fundamentalism, particularly ecofundamentalism or environmental fundamentalism. Of course, it whole-heartedly embraces the natural sciences and usually defends the natural rights of all human beings. Yet, it rejects other modern developments and provides alternatives. It despises the limitless use of *technè* in the form of the systematic exploitation of the natural world causing pollution, reduction of biodiversity, deforestation, and human-induced climate change.

The second class of properties characterizing fundamentalisms concerns the fact that, paradoxically, they are themselves highly modern phenomena, as has been pointed out in the literature (e.g., Bendroth 2014, 56; Clarke 2017, 61; Harding 2000, 270; Krüger 2006, 886; Williamson 2020, 41). Perhaps most eloquent is Bruce Lawrence, who says that fundamentalists are "moderns, but not modernists" and "at once the consequence of modernity and the antithesis of modernism" (Lawrence 1989, 2). This, of course, raises the question of what modernity is. Charles Taylor's influential account says it is a distinct culture that includes, among other things, a growth of science, individualism, instrumental reason searching for and imposing certainty and control, and negative freedom (freedom as freedom from various impediments), as well as a particular moral outlook on the world that comes with specific understandings of persons, nature, society, and the good (see Taylor 1989, 1995, 27–8). The search for certainty and control can take different shapes, but a stereotypical one found in funda-mentalisms is a literal-historical reading of entire holy scriptures that are

---

[18] See, respectively, www.icr.org and https://creation.com/journal-of-creation-archive-index.

deemed infallible, indubitable, or inerrable: the Koran, the sharia, the First and Second Testaments (that is, the Bible), the halakha, the Talmud, and the Guru Granth Sahib. Perhaps this applies even, to some extent, to such secular texts as Marx's *Das Kapital* when leaders like Lenin permit only their own interpretation of these texts. Of course, things are slightly more complex here: even early fundamentalists did not read the entirety of the Bible literally. They did not think that God is literally a rock, that he has hands, or that Christ is a loaf of bread. But core passages that were and are usually read as more metaphorical were read by fundamentalists as representing a literal-historical and sometimes even scientific reality. Creationist readings of Genesis 1–3 are undoubtedly the most well-known example of this. This approach to holy scriptures is rarely found before modernity. Literal-historical readings of the Bible are largely absent before the Reformation, for instance. They discard any kind of modern hermeneutics that pays attention to gender, layers of meanings in texts, the semantic horizons of a culture, and the position of the reader. Such certainty can also be found in the formulation of external fundamentals or in the charisma of leaders.

Another, more practical and straightforward way in which many fundamentalist movements are modern is that they employ modern means of communication, especially when they have a missionary drive. Examples are the use of social media by creationist movements and the high-quality videos made by Islamist fundamentalists, such as ISIS's utterly cruel videos of executions.[19]

A final characteristic of fundamentalist movements that has to do with modernity is that their truth claims are particularly modern. They are neither premodern (such truth claims are sometimes local or tribal) nor postmodern (such truth claims are often subjective or relative). Fundamentalists make universal claims about truths in ethics, regulations for the good life, and diagnoses of what is wrong with the world. The idea that multiple perspectives may hold important insights is rejected.

This brings us to the third type of properties: fundamentalist movements embrace an overarching narrative about the world that usually has two dimensions. The one dimension is historical: there once was a perfectly good paradisaical state, that state was lost due to a fall, and we now need to restore the original perfectly good state. This historical narrative plays out in different ways. There is, of course, the literal-historical understanding of Genesis 1–3, in which Adam and Eve lost the paradise in the Garden of Eden by eating from the forbidden fruit, thereby violating God's explicit commandment. But the same pattern can be found in, say, Wahhabism: the caliphate was the original and

---

[19] For use of digital media among religious fundamentalist millennials and so-called zoomers (generations Y and Z), see Missier (2022).

good state, it was destroyed by human sin, and it now needs to be brought back. We even witness a version of this pattern in neo-Nazism: European countries, particularly what they call the boreal countries, were once populated by Caucasians, but things went radically wrong with mass immigration after World War II. We need to restore the original peaceful and prosperous situation in which Europe was all White.

The other dimension of this narrative is of a more metaphysical kind, often referred to as *moral dualism*. The fundamental idea is that there are two forces in the world, those of good and evil, which battle for dominance. There is nothing in between: one is either on the good side or on the bad side (see Almond, Sivan, and Appleby 1995, 406; Clarke 2017, 50).[20] The militant fundamentalist and separatist Carl McIntire, for instance, who was the editor of the Christian magazine *Beacon*, says, in his strident book *Twentieth Century Reformation*: "It is the age-long battle in which we are now engaged, right inside the church— it is light versus darkness" (McIntire 1945, 212). This is important, for it means that even the tiniest of our actions has universal value—after all, it has a place in this cosmic battle. This is frequently tied to othering and animosity toward those outside of the group: they are godless, sinful, contaminated, or even doomed to condemnation. This moral dualism or black-and-white thinking often gets a particularly sharp edge when it is wed to an eschatological vision in terms of messianism, millenarianism, or apocalypticism.[21]

A significant advantage of this analysis of fundamentalism in terms of stereotypical properties is that it can make sense of the fact that, both in academic and in public discourse, two movements can be described as funda- mentalist even if they hold opposite views and engage in contradictory prac- tices. For instance, dance is a core religious practice in Haredi Judaism, but it was considered godless by early twentieth-century Christian fundamentalists. Right-wing Islamophobic extremists can be fundamentalist, while Salafi jihad- ists, who believe that the whole world is to be violently conquered and subju- gated to Allah, are also fundamentalists.

It is important to note which properties are characteristic of fundamentalism, but it is almost as important to note which ones are apparently not. The use or support of *violence* is not one of the stereotypical properties of fundamentalism —pace authors like Sathianathan Clarke (2017). It is somewhat more accurate

---

[20] This is sometimes referred to as *moral Manicheism* (e.g., Almond, Appleby, and Sivan 2003, 95). I will not use that expression, since Manicheism taught that there is good in evil and vice versa and that good and evil are two equally powerful sources in the world—two things that funda- mentalisms generally deny.

[21] This list of properties also squares well with recent quantitative research, for example, by the Pew Research Center in their *Religious Landscape Study* (2014), in which self-identified nondenominational fundamentalists filled in a questionnaire.

to say that *militancy* is a stereotypical property, as long as one notes that militancy can take all sorts of nonviolent forms, such as a particular rhetoric and specific tactics. Joel Carpenter (1997, 64), for instance, says that "militancy was the mark of fundamentalism, and ideological militancy especially," and George Marsden (1980, 4) understands fundamentalism as "militant opposition to modernism." Others have argued that even militancy is not that typical of fundamentalism (Crawford 2014, 43; Hood, Hill, and Williamson 2005). Christian fundamentalism, for example, has not always been militant, even though it was during the first years, partially because of the war rhetoric that still permeated society after World War I. As Watt has argued in detail, the second wave of Christian fundamentalists, which included figures such as Harold Ockenga, intentionally adopted a more irenic approach and rejected the discursive combative militancy and aggression of their predecessors, such as J. Frank Norris and John Roach Straton. For instance, they avoided the warfare metaphors used by the early proponents, who employed such words as *battle royal*, *crusade*, and *skirmish* (Watt 2014, 23, 31).

I have also not included *organizational characteristics*, such as charismatic leadership and authoritarian structures, among the stereotypical properties of fundamentalisms.[22] Of course, many fundamentalist movements have these properties, but then so do cults, extremist movements, fanaticist movements, and conspiracist groups. The same holds for various *affective elements*, like fear and hostility—these are also insufficiently distinctive of fundamentalism. Finally, I have not included the idea that fundamentalists are *certain* or *highly certain* of their doctrines or beliefs. As several authors have pointed out, "strongly agree" responses on surveys may well be explained by a social desirability response bias or even a doctrinal desirability response bias (Rouse et al. 2019, 291–2). The fact that many fundamentalists articulate what they consider to be fundamental principles and seek control perhaps suggests that they in fact lack subjective certainty in these core doctrinal statements, as I have pointed out elsewhere (Peels and Kindermann 2022). Liht and others even define *fundamentalism* as "the form that religion takes when it becomes uncertain about itself" (Liht et al. 2011, 300).[23]

The stereotypical properties described here are jointly distinctive of fundamentalism. This analysis, in conjunction with our brief characterization of monotheism in the Introduction, already provides a few insights into the

---

[22] For properties like these, see the description in Almond, Appleby, and Sivan (2003, 97–115).

[23] This may be confirmed by the finding of Hunsberger et al. (1996) that low fundamentalists—those who score low on fundamentalism scales—turn out to have more doubts about God and religion than high fundamentalists—those who score high on such tests—who seem to solve their doubts in a religious direction.

relations between the two. Most scholars understand fundamentalism as, para-doxically, a modern response to modern phenomena.[24] But of course, most monotheisms that we mentioned existed prior to modernity. This means that monotheism can come, and often has come, without fundamentalism. It may have come with violence, with othering, with moral dualism, and the like, but some core characteristics of fundamentalism are absent from most of the history of most monotheisms. In other words, monotheism has existed without fundamentalism for most of its history. Monotheism can entail or raise the likelihood of fundamentalism only when conjoined with particular histor-ical, political, and cultural developments found in modernity, late modernity in particular. Moreover, we saw that our family resemblance analysis implies that diametrically opposed movements can be equally fundamental-ist, such as left-wing radical environmentalism or ecofundamentalism on the one hand and capitalist fundamentalism on the other, or neo-Nazism or fascism on the one hand and certain versions of Marxism and communism on the other. This means that if fundamentalism is prevalent in monotheism, it is perfectly possible that it is equally or even more prevalent in, say, polytheistic or secular worldviews. We will explore this issue in more depth in the next section.

Finally, specific fundamentalist movements comprise not only beliefs but also affections, such as fears, angers, and grievances. They also come with conative states—that is, certain goals, desires, and intentions. Moreover, they have certain structures related to charisma and hierarchical organizations, and they come with material and abstract objects, such as flags and symbols. This means that accounts of specific fundamentalist movements merely in terms of beliefs, belief systems, or "attitudes about one's religious beliefs"[25] are falling short. We should not overrationalize fundamentalism: on the group level it comes with beliefs, but that is not the whole story.

1.5 Positionality and the Study of Fundamentalism

How one carries out the study of fundamentalism depends on one's particular political, cultural, moral, social, economic, epistemic, and religious perspective and context. In other words, it has to do with one's positionality. This does not defeat the academic value of such work, but it calls for awareness of and reflection on one's own position. Positionality enters the debate in different ways, a couple of which I would like to mention here.

---

[24] There are a few exceptions, such as Denemark (2008, 579); Jones (2010, 220).

[25] The latter would problematically imply that fundamentalism is a meta-attitude: it would be not so much a set of beliefs as an attitude toward one's beliefs.

If being a fundamentalist movement is indeed a matter of exemplifying *enough of* the stereotypical properties that I described, then it will vary from person to person what they consider as "enough." Not only that, it will also differ how much relative weight is attached to each of these properties. Some would say, for instance, that whether or not a movement is reactive toward modernity carries more weight than whether or not it employs modern means of communication.[26] Positionality also has to do with where one starts in analyzing and studying fundamentalism: Does one start from a particular conception of what fundamentalism is or from particular cases that one considers to be prime examples of fundamentalism? This is the so-called problem of the criterion (see Chisholm 1973). Where one starts may often matter for where one ends up. Positionality is crucial here, for instance, because it has been argued that the examples adduced to study fundamentalism have been unduly Western centered, but clearly, positionality is equally present if one starts from a particular conception of fundamentalism.

So let me be frank and put my cards on the table. I am an academic, trained in analytic philosophy and theology. I am a Christian, raised in the Reformed tradition but by now equally comfortable—particularly liturgically—in the Anglican, Roman Catholic, and Eastern Orthodox churches. Belief in God permeates the entirety of my life and is the very foundation of it. I am regularly struck by a deep sense of both aesthetic and religious wonder and awe. I am an epistemic and moral realist. I am a White male European, deeply shaped not only by the Judeo-Christian tradition but also by the secular intellectual climate that surrounds me in Amsterdam and the Netherlands more generally. I have been formed by life in a multicultural society and an often antagonistic and increasingly polarized political climate. I have always lived in urban rather than rural areas. I am married to my wife and have children. All these things undoubtedly exercise an influence on how I think of monotheism and fundamentalism. I have intentionally sought to counter potential confirmation biases and other biases I may have in this regard; for example, I have requested feedback on this manuscript from colleagues in and beyond philosophy and theology whose gender, life orientation, and circumstances are different from mine.

1.6 Conclusion

This section started by pointing out that *fundamentalism* is a highly controversial term—in fact, so controversial that many scholars advocate abandoning it altogether. I argued that there is much to be gained from using the term,

---

[26] In fact, some might suggest that the very idea that fundamentalism is reactive toward modernity itself shows positionality, because it takes modernity as a given and fundamentalism as a reactive movement rather than taking modernity as a phenomenon that is also shaped by its response to fundamentalism (for this point, see Williamson 2020, 43).

especially when it comes to spotting similarities across otherwise radically different fundamentalist movements. That said, use of the term comes with certain risks. In what follows, at each juncture, we will have to be sensitive to crucial differences between religious and secular fundamentalist movements, between several religious and in particular Abrahamic fundamentalisms, and, in fact, between numerous movements within specific religions. Needless to say, various traits of fundamentalism are widely—maybe particularly in academia—considered to be epistemically or morally problematic, such as its dismissal of science and its treatment of women and sexual minorities. But that should not blind us to the fact that in some ways, fundamentalisms may be harmless or even benign.

2 How Prevalent Is Fundamentalism in Monotheism?

2.1 Introduction

In the previous section, we saw that various authors boldly state that monotheism leads to fundamentalism, violence, intolerance, and other related phenomena. But exactly what is the evidence for such sweeping statements? Few of these authors level anything at all to back up such claims. We live in polarized times, particularly when it comes to religion and other life orientations, and such statements ought to be made only if we can actually show that they hold water. In this section, therefore, we delve into the empirical dimension of the relation between monotheism and fundamentalism.

We do so in two ways. First, we consider whether there is empirical evidence for a relation between monotheistic thinking and fundamentalist mindsets. Second, we examine how prevalent fundamentalism is in monotheism. How contextual is this prevalence? In other words, how much does it vary from one political and cultural context to another, both geographically and historically? Do we have any quantitative data about this that are sufficiently reliable? And how prevalent is it comparatively, both among various monotheisms and in monotheistic religions in comparison with polytheistic religions and secular worldviews? The question of how monotheism relates to fundamentalism from an empirical point of view is so large that it is hardly ever addressed in the literature. The bird's-eye perspective that we adopt here is rather sketchy, but as we shall see, it allows us to make some important observations about how monotheism relates to fundamentalism.

2.2 Measuring Fundamentalism

If we want to make any concrete statements about the empirical relation between monotheism and fundamentalism, ideally, we should be able to operationalize and measure that relation. In the literature, we find four distinct ways of measuring the prevalence of fundamentalism in a population.[27] Let us consider these four options in some detail.

(1) Some studies assume that (religious) fundamentalism can be operationalized by way of a single characteristic thought to be typical of fundamentalism, such as the claim that there is only one true way to interpret one's religion (Beller and Kröger 2021, 557), biblical literalism (Chung et al. 2019, 379), biblical inerrancy (Sherkat and Darnell 1999, 28), or high religious commitment (Grigoropoulos 2014, 203). The problem with this approach is that, while such properties may well be characteristic of fundamentalism, they are often equally found beyond fundamentalism. Many nonfundamentalists, for instance, are also highly committed to their religion or think their holy scriptures are infallible. These operationalizations, then, are insufficiently detailed and therefore extensionally inaccurate.

(2) Other studies assume that a certain classification in an existing dataset entails being a fundamentalist, such as belonging to a particular religious denomination. The problem with such an approach is that it faces well-known worries. It is known from social epistemology that a group can believe something even if many or even all of its members do not believe it.[28] Similarly, a denomination may well be fundamentalist—say, because its main representatives or operative members embrace fundamentalist positions and policies—while many other members of that denomination are not themselves fundamentalist. One can, of course, also classify a denomination as fundamentalist because most of its members are fundamentalist, but in that case, one needs to know how many of its members are actually fundamentalist—so, one will have to resort to another method.

(3) Another way to measure fundamentalism is to use the self-identifications of subjects in questionnaires as indicator of fundamentalism (e.g., Alwin et al. 2006; Beyerlein 2004; Streyffeler and McNally 1998). Thus, individuals are asked questions such as this: "When it comes to your religious identity, would you say you are a Pentecostal, fundamentalist, evangelical, mainline, or liberal Protestant, or do none of these describe you?" An obvious problem with this approach is the pejorative meaning or negative connotation of the term *fundamentalist* in ordinary discourse. Subjects, then, may well not self-identify as fundamentalist even though they are in fact fundamentalists on most accounts of fundamentalism. Florian Pohl (2014, 226) goes so far as to say that "fundamentalism rarely, if ever, constitutes an element of self-identification but is used to describe the 'other.'"

---

[27] For helpful input and conversations on these four ways, I thank Nora Kindermann.

[28] I myself have argued this also holds for ignorance: groups can be ignorant of something even if all of their members know it. See Peels (2023a).

(4) Finally, some authors have provided their own operationalizations of fundamentalism, often by presenting subjects either with statements they can rate (Examples 1–4) or with pairs of Bible citations (Example 5):

1. The *Revised Religious Fundamentalism Scale* was developed by Bob Altemeyer and Bruce Hunsberger (2004). It is a revision of their original Religious Fundamentalism Scale (Altemeyer and Hunsberger 1992), which consisted of twenty items; the revised scale has twelve. In both cases, subjects were asked to indicate on a scale ranging from –4 ("very strongly disagree") to +4 ("very strongly agree") how much they agreed with each statement.

2. The *Intratextual Fundamentalism Scale*, developed by Paul Williamson and others (Williamson et al. 2010), is a five-item cross-cultural scale, tested on Islamic and Christian samples of students in Pakistan and the United States. It is designed to avoid any content bias or concern for aggression. The idea of the former is that it zooms out from beliefs of particular fundamentalisms to identify commonalities in attitudes across different fundamentalist movements. It zooms in on intratextuality—the idea that objective truth can best be discovered by consulting only the sacred text—as opposed to intertextuality—the idea that objective truth can best be discovered by also consulting other texts, such as texts from science, history, archeology, and scholarly criticism.

3. The *Multidimensional Fundamentalism Inventory*, developed by José Liht and others (Liht et al. 2011), is one of the few scales specifically designed to also measure non-Christian varieties of fundamentalism, namely, those in Judaism and Islam. It is based on American samples (college students) and Mexican samples (broader samples) and works with a three-component structure, each component consisting of five items. Here are the components with, by way of example, one item for each of them: (1) External versus internal authority—for instance, "I admire those who leave their ideas behind and submit to God's will"; (2) Fixed versus malleable religion—for instance, "True religion never changes"; and (3) Worldly rejection versus worldly affirmation—for instance, "It is important to distance oneself from movies, radio, and TV."

4. The *North American Protestant Fundamentalism Scale*, developed by James Deal and Karin Bartoszuk (2014), is a four-component scale in terms of inerrancy of scripture, evangelism, premillennialism or rapture theology, and separatism, based on Nancy T. Ammerman's work on North American Protestant fundamentalism. The study, which has a twenty-three-item list, is based on online surveys among students at two American state universities.

5. The *Bible Verse Selection Task* was developed by Steven Rouse and others (Rouse et al. 2019) to measure specifically Christian fundamentalism. Students at religiously affiliated universities were invited to select out of 100 Bible verses

those that they deemed most central to their faith. The twelve Bible verses associated with Christian fundamentalism were then paired with other biblical texts and presented to Amazon Mechanical Turk workers in the United States, asking them to indicate which ones were more central to their faith. Their responses were used to develop the Bible Verse Selection Task. The authors preferred this over Likert-type formats, in which subjects are asked to indicate their level of agreement with various doctrinal statements, primarily because of potential social desirability response bias. They claim that such bias is less salient in their Bible Verse Selection Task and that the measurement does equally well on criterion-related validity and construct validity.

These five scales are among the most influential in the study of fundamentalism: they have often been used and, in some cases, even been adapted to be applied in different contexts, such as the Intratextual Fundamentalism Scale to Muslims in Indonesia (e.g., Muluk, Sumaktoyo, and Ruth 2013). They do well in terms of their psychometric properties (mean interim correlation, alpha reliability, etc.), internal consistency, empirical validity, and construct validity, and many of them show interesting correlations with fundamentalism-related phenomena such as belief in creation science, racial prejudice, dogmatism, and right-wing authoritarianism.[29] For this reason, such operationalizations are to be preferred over the three other ways to attempt to measure fundamentalism. Given the many agreements between the family resemblance account of fundamentalism provided in Section 1 and the ideas about fundamentalism underlying scales like these, they can be fruitfully used to measure fundamentalism.

This is not to deny that serious questions can be asked about these studies. For instance, some of them work solely with university students. However, can we easily generalize from the ensuing data to whether or not others who have not received university education—the majority of fundamentalists, it seems—are also fundamentalist? Moreover, many of these scales need to be reconsidered in light of more-detailed accounts of fundamentalism. It has struck me that several scales work with a somewhat primitive, undeveloped notion of fundamentalism that leads to various questionable items on their lists. By way of example, consider the following four items:

- No one religion is especially close to God, nor does God favor any particular group of believers (no. 10 on the original scale in Altemeyer and Hunsberger [1992]).
- Whenever science and sacred scripture conflict, *science* is probably right (no. 10 on the new scale in Altemeyer and Hunsberger [2004]).

---

[29] That is, in the contexts in which these scales were tested.

- We should all rejoice when a new believer is welcomed into the family of God.
- The Bible is true in a way that other holy books are not.[30]

It is questionable whether these items or their negations are in any way indicative of fundamentalism. It is part and parcel of Judaism, for instance, that the people of Israel *are* especially close to God—they are supposed to be the light of the nations. Similarly, it is constitutive of Islam that God favors Muslims—those who confess the *shahadah* that "there is no true god but Allah, and Muhammad is the Messenger of God." As to the second item, many mainstream religious believers, particularly orthodox ones, take it that if science and sacred scripture conflict, science must be wrong, but that most such alleged conflicts are cases in which we have apparently *misinterpreted* scripture. In those cases, denial of the second item is hardly indicative of fundamentalism—probably rather the opposite, given the hermeneutical sensitivity involved. Negative scores on the first and second items are therefore questionable indicators of fundamentalism. The third and fourth items seem part of mainstream Christianity: Why would a Christian not rejoice when someone converts to Christianity? And, of course, many Christians ascribe a truth status to the Bible that they do not ascribe to the Koran or the Hadith.

2.3 Monotheistic and Fundamentalist Thinking

Now, can these fundamentalism scales be used to establish the empirical relation between monotheism and fundamentalism? That is questionable, for two reasons.

First, these fundamentalism scales have been designed to measure the degree of fundamentalism among specific populations. In fact, some of them say *expressis verbis* that they measure only *religious* fundamentalism. Others do not say this but clearly operationalize only religious varieties of fundamentalism. Another important problem is that these scales have been designed and used in Western contexts. But obviously, there is fundamentalism far beyond the Western world. This is, in fact, a more general problem with many studies in psychology and sociology, as the "beyond WEIRD" studies—where the acronym stands for Western, Educated, Industrialized, Rich, and Democratic—have pointed out: many studies suffer from a lack of sample diversity, and there is, therefore, insufficient reason to think that their results are representative of *Homo sapiens* (see, e.g., Apicella, Norenzayan, and Henrich 2020). Thus, these scales often cannot be used without qualification and revision in non-Western

---

[30] The third and fourth items are from Deal and Bartoszuk (2014).

contexts—if they can be used there at all. It follows that, as things stand, these scales cannot be used to measure whether there is a correlation between monotheistic and fundamentalist thinking or mindsets or what the percentage of fundamentalists is in various religious and other worldviews.

Second, the methods laid out in these fundamentalism scales have been used to measure fundamentalism only in smaller groups, such as certain Baptist denominations in the United States. It will be hard, if not impossible, to use them for such groups as all Muslims on earth, given the many subtle differences in religious doctrine and practice, nationality, language, tradition, and much more that need to be considered in order to measure the ratio of fundamentalism within a particular monotheistic tradition. Thus, at this stage, we cannot confer any precise numbers to the proportion of fundamentalists in mainstream Abrahamic religions.

Should we, then, give up on the project of exploring the empirical relation between fundamentalism and monotheism? Not yet. Even if we cannot confer any precise number, we can rely on the literature to see how widespread fundamentalism actually is both within and beyond monotheistic religions. These are global observations and rough estimates, but they are better than nothing, particularly when it comes to assessing sweeping claims about the relation between monotheism and fundamentalism.

2.4 Fundamentalism in Christianity

Let us start our exploration of fundamentalism in Christianity with Roman Catholicism.[31] Roman Catholicism has many properties that are often associated with fundamentalism: for example, it has a single leader, and it is rather strict about doctrine (in theory at least). Yet it is near universally agreed that there is little fundamentalism in the Roman Catholic Church. According to Michał Gierycz (2020), Catholicism "is not a fertile soil for fundamentalism in the political sense of the term, despite the strict Catholic dogmatics, its monotheism, a single leader who provides the ultimate and binding interpretation of the truths of faith (see the dogma of papal infallibility in matters of faith and morals), as well as the hierarchical structure of power and subordination."

This is probably due to further characteristics of the Roman Catholic Church, to which we return in Section 4: it confers great authority upon tradition (which has, among other things, largely a nonliteral reading of the Bible and opponents different from modernity), it has a universal and global orientation, and so on. That said, fundamentalist groups can still be found in the Roman Catholic

---

[31] For thoughts and suggestions regarding fundamentalism in Roman Catholicism, I thank Marcel Sarot.

Church. Among the groups often considered to be fundamentalist are Opus Dei, which has some 95,000 members, and Comunione e Liberazione, with some 300,000 members—certainly not insignificant, but relatively small in a church with approximately 1.3 billion members.

What about Eastern Orthodox churches? Most of these churches, such as the Albanian Orthodox Church, are undoubtedly conservative—for instance, when it comes to homosexuality or the rights of women. Yet, it seems that, overall, it would be mistaken to classify them as fundamentalist, because they take a nuanced position toward modernity, acknowledge subtlety and nuance in the moral realm, and so forth. A notable and crucial exception to this is the Russian Orthodox Church, also known as the Moscow patriarchate. It currently has some 110 million members, most of whom reside in Russia—about half of 220 million Eastern Orthodox Christians worldwide. Under the patriarchy of Kirill, this church has radicalized over the last few years. Kirill has blessed soldiers and their weapons in the war against Ukraine and fulminated against the many sins of the West, gay prides in particular. In response to the decision of the ecumenical patriarch in Constantinople to grant autocephaly (independence) to the Orthodox Church of Ukraine, there was a schism with the patriarchate of Constantinople. The Russian Orthodox Church has ever held close ties with the Kremlin, especially with President Vladimir Putin, culminating in full support for and religious justification of the horrendous war against Ukraine. Kirill also repeated Putin's claim that Ukraine is ruled by fascists and promised eternal life to all Russians who would die fighting in Ukraine. The racism, anti-Semitism, othering, and call for violence are blatant and rampant, even though there is also some opposition to these things within the Russian Orthodox Church.

Let us briefly turn to Protestantism. Fundamentalism is a prominent phenomenon in Protestant churches. We already saw that it first arose among early twentieth-century conservative evangelicals in the United States. At the time, however, they formed a minority among Protestants: "Most members of the Assemblies of God, the Church of the Nazarene, the National Baptist Convention, the Southern Baptist Convention, the Churches of Christ, and the Missouri Synod of the Lutheran Church were not a part of the fundamentalist coalition" (Watt 2014, 32). Nowadays, we find fundamentalists among Baptists, Mennonites, evangelicals, and Jehovah's Witnesses, as well as within the Alliance Church.

Exactly what percentage of Protestants is fundamentalist is hard to tell, but there are good reasons to think that fundamentalists still form a minority. First, by far the largest groups of Protestants consist of Pentecostals and charismatics, and these believers are usually not considered fundamentalist (e.g., Bendroth

2014, 58). They are found in thousands of smaller independent denominational organizations, and there are some 520 million of them now, about one third of Christians worldwide and possibly soon the largest group of Christians on earth. They are not considered fundamentalist because of such things as the emphasis on personal encounters with the Holy Spirit, the additional value experience is thought to have next to scripture, and the central importance of healing and prophecy. Furthermore, Pentecostalist and charismatic movements often have their roots in old, local traditions in the Southern Hemisphere, whereas fundamentalism is a highly modernist phenomenon.

Second, fundamentalism is also rare in other large churches that are considered Protestant, such as the Anglican Church (some 85 million members) and the Lutheran Church (some 77 million members). Their global orientation and, for the Anglican Church, its more hierarchical organization may be important explanatory factors here. Evolutionary theory, female leadership, and more liberal ethics are now widely accepted in these churches.[32]

Christianity consists largely of Roman Catholicism, Protestantism (including Pentecostalism and charismatic movements), and the Orthodox Church. Since fundamentalists form a minority in each of these, the only reasonable conclusion is that fundamentalism is a minority position in Christianity.

2.5 Fundamentalism in Islam

Let us now turn to Islam. Islam was the second religion for which the term *fundamentalism* was used, particularly since the Iranian revolution, which led to the overthrow of the Pahlavi dynasty in 1979. It is the second-largest religion on earth, with some 1.6 billion believers. Islam is obviously dominant in the Middle East, but there are also many Muslims living in the Asia-Pacific region, the countries with the three largest Muslim populations being Indonesia, India, and Pakistan. Historically deeply influenced by Judaism and Christianity—the other religions of the book—Islam yet differs from them in that, from the very start, it was not just a religious but also a social, economic, and political movement (Clarke 2017, 69). It is quite common in the literature to speak of *Islamic fundamentalism, political Islam, Islamism, jihadism,* or *Islamic radicalism.*[33] Some of these terms denote phenomena that are not just fundamentalist but also extremist or even terrorist. Here, we zoom in on instances of fundamentalism. Of course, fundamentalism in Islam is partially rather different from fundamentalism in Christianity. Liberal theology, for instance, is an almost

---

[32] Fundamentalism is a prominent phenomenon in the United States. We should not forget, though, that only some 20 percent of Protestants live in the United States.

[33] For elucidation of these terms, see Choueiri (2010).

negligible phenomenon in Islam, and Islamic fundamentalists, therefore, do not primarily react to liberal theology. We also find shared characteristics, though, such as anti-modernism, an emphasis on classical family values, traditional gender roles, and cosmic dualism.

Now, what percentage of Muslims can rightly be considered fundamentalist? A crucial distinction when it comes to fundamentalism and Islam is that between the Sunni and Shia branches, which have some 1.4 billion and 160–210 million believers, respectively. This distinction matters, among other things, because Shias constitute a small minority within Islam, forming the majority only in a couple of countries, such as Iran, Azerbaijan, Bahrain, and Iraq. Minorities can turn fundamentalist partly as a result of reacting toward the majority. But majorities can also turn fundamentalist—for instance, as a result of colonialization or perceived Western dominance.

Perhaps the best-known example of Sunni-based fundamentalism is the Muslim Brotherhood in Egypt. Egypt has been part of the Ottoman Empire, it has been under French colonial rule, and it has been under direct British political influence as a British protectorate between 1914 and 1922. The embodiment of modernity in Egypt was the completion of the Suez Canal in 1869, a project on which the French and the Egyptians closely cooperated. Like Christian fundamentalism, the Muslim Brotherhood first surfaced in the 1920s.[34] Founded by Hassan al-Banna in 1928, it opposed Gamal Abdel Nasser's secular rule and grew in the sixties partly due to the writings of Sayyid Qutb, who was first imprisoned and then killed by Nasser in 1966. Qutb's ideas, particularly his violent opposition to the Western world and secular governments in the Middle East that in his view embodied the same mindset, are still championed by many Islamic fundamentalists today. In 2012, the Muslim Brotherhood, represented by Mohamed Morsi, gained political power and kept it for only a year. Morsi was sentenced to death, and the Muslim Brotherhood is suppressed nowadays. It inspired the Salafi (from *al-salafiyyah*) movement, which is said to constitute no more than 1 percent of Muslims worldwide.[35] Yet things are complicated, because even within Salafism, we find quietism and political activism. In fact, some have argued that most Salafis either support the existing governments or are apolitical (Blankinship 2014, 150, 152).

Ever since the turn of the twenty-first century, some Islamic fundamentalist movements, such as the Muslim Brotherhood, have grown from thinking nationally to thinking globally. In fact, this may be another way in which fundamentalist movements can be typically modern. An infamous example of

---

[34] This is rightly noted by Clarke (2017, 65).

[35] Thus Livesey (2005). For more on the Muslim Brotherhood, see Wagemakers (2020).

this is IS (also ISIS or ISIL), which, by way of extreme violence, has pursued the establishment of a caliphate. It considers itself a Sunni-based movement and seeks to return to an idealized past in which there were no borders between nation-states and all Muslims jointly formed the *ummah*, the worldwide religious community. IS has accomplished this in large parts of Syria and Iraq, using modern weapons and modern media. Similar in many ways is Boko Haram, which is active in northeastern Nigeria, Chad, Niger, and Cameroon. Its name is already indicative of its reactive nature: it means "Western education is fraud."

Muslim fundamentalists have sought to implement sharia as the basis of individual human behavior, social relationships in groups, and the organization of the state. Human events are seen as immutable signs of God's will. They embrace a strong us-versus-them thinking, sometimes paired with violence, both toward non-Muslims and toward nonradical Muslims. The world is a cosmic battle between *hizb Allah* (the party of God) and *hizb al-shaytan* (the party of Satan); there is nothing in between. In trying to build a Muslim *ummah*, Muslim fundamentalists are combative and expansionist. They oppose and fight not just the secular West but also modern and secular governments and developments in the Arab world.

Another variety of Sunni fundamentalism is to be found in Wahhabism or Salafism—the two terms are often used interchangeably—for instance, in Saudi Arabia. Based on the doctrines of Islamic preacher and theologian Muhammad Ibn Abd al-Wahhab (1703–92), Salafism is a reformist movement that seeks to return to the alleged purity of the first three generations (*salaf*). It emphasizes the *zahir*—that is, the literal or apparent—meaning of the Koran and the Hadith, and it is opposed to mysticism and Shia Islam, as some beliefs and practices in the latter are thought to conflict with monotheism. While Salafism embraces certain parts of modernity, such as technological developments, it is highly critical of numerous other elements of particularly Western modernity, such as ideologies like liberalism and socialism, ideas in science that are thought to conflict with Islamic doctrine, and equal rights for women.

Iran is another country in which a significant portion of the population can rightly be considered fundamentalist. Here, however, it is Shia rather than Sunni fundamentalism that is dominant. Even within Iran, Shia fundamentalists come in many shapes and sizes: conservative fundamentalists, traditionalist fundamentalists, radical fundamentalists, and so on. Iranian fundamentalists often call themselves *principalists*—that is, people acting on Islamic and revolutionary principles. Ruhollah Khomeini, known as Ayatollah Khomeini, led the Iranian revolution in 1979. Under his leadership until 1989, political Islam was formally accepted as the ideology of the country, public law sanctioning sinful behavior and encouraging pious behavior. Iranian fundamentalism manifests itself in such things as the following: It confers fewer rights on people of other faiths. For instance, secular persons are not allowed to enter university or be on a city council, and hundreds of mystical Sufi Muslims have been arrested. Those considered to be blasphemous can be publicly executed, and scholars and theologians who oppose official ideology are often imprisoned. The West is considered the primary enemy because of its politics, its culture (such as the prominence of music), and particularly its liberal ethics—Iran has publicly hanged numerous homosexuals over the last few decades. The rights of women are severely restricted. They are subject to strict dress codes, frequently checked upon by Iranian police. The ideal portrayed for women is to be a wife and mother, and they are disadvantaged in legal systems, such as inheritance laws. The supreme leader is thought to be both holy and infallible. His legitimacy and authority are given by God, not by the people.

These are just some examples. Muslim fundamentalism can be found among most followers of Qutb, Khomeini, and Abu al-A 'la al-Mawdudi in numerous movements and countries. It can also be found in organizations and movements that are not just fundamentalist but also extremist, such as the Taliban—with regional aspirations—and Al Qaeda—with global aspirations. Scholars agree that these movements all ought to be qualified as fundamentalist and extremist, sometimes even as terrorist.

Yet one may wonder whether the percentage of fundamentalists among Muslims is perhaps much larger than the proportion of these movements in Islam. After all, do not most Muslims embrace rather traditional gender roles, reject homosexuality, take the Koran to be infallible, and believe that Islam is the only true religion? I think there is a kernel of truth in this: the percentage of liberal Muslims in Islam is much smaller than the percentage of liberal believers in Christianity or Judaism. However, we should not confuse fundamentalism with something like conservatism or orthodoxy, as Bassam Tibi (2013, 17) writes: "A major flaw of the prevailing narrative is its failure to recognize Islamism as a variety of the phenomenon of religious fundamentalism. Thus, it is not a conservatism. To be sure, Islamic conservatism and Islamic fundamentalism are not the same and should not be confused." In Section 1, we already saw that a movement counts as fundamentalist only if it exemplifies a sufficiently large number of the stereotypical properties; just having one or two will not do, because that will capture also different phenomena, things such as conservatism and orthodoxy. The percentage of conservatives and orthodox within Islam is much higher than that in Christianity or Judaism. That said, it does not follow that Islam as a whole is more fundamentalist. To get to fundamentalism, we need to add various properties that many Muslims appear to lack—things like cosmic dualism and the othering of nonbelievers (e.g., atheists or members of animist religions in Sudan).[36]

2.6 Fundamentalism in Judaism

Jewish fundamentalism is quite different from Christian and Islamic fundamentalism. Given the emphasis on oral tradition in Judaism generally, the idea of literalism in interpreting scriptures is largely absent. And the main Jewish movement in which we do find such literalism—Karaism—is widely considered not to be fundamentalist.

It is quite customary to distinguish three groups of fundamentalists in Judaism: the Hasidim, the non-Hasidic ultra-Orthodox Jews (or strict Orthodox Jews), and the religious or nonreligious ultranationalists among Zionist settlers. That said, some avidly deny that the term *fundamentalism* can fruitfully be used for the third group. The term *Haredi Judaism* is often used to refer to both the first and second groups. There is opposition between various of these groups; for instance, between Satmar Hasidim and Habad Hasidim (also called Chabad or Lubavitch), as well as between Satmar Hasidim and Zionists (Magid 2014a, 70–1). In fact, some have argued that the first and second groups, on the one hand, and the third group, on the other, are diametrically opposed (Cahan 2014, 109). In the general group of religious ultranationalism, we find specific groups that are often considered fundamentalist, such as the Hilltop Youth, Gush Emunim, and the Kach party.

What renders these movements fundamentalist differs quite a bit among them. For Habad Hasidism, it is messianic activism, what some qualify as "spiritual racism"[37] and strong anti-modernism, at least when it comes to such things as ethical positions (their media and music are rather modern, but we already saw that this is often the case with fundamentalism). Satmar Hasidism was originally founded by Rabbi Teitelbaum (1878–1979). It is now well known from its depiction in the 2020 four-part television miniseries *Unorthodox*, which was loosely based on Deborah Feldman's 2012 autobiography *Unorthodox: The Scandalous Rejection of My Hasidic Roots*. In this movement, Zionism and secularism are considered to be foes because they are perceived as attempts to bring about our own redemption by earthly, political means. Satmar Hasidism sticks to the traditional Jewish view, which was mainstream until 1945, that the return to the land of Israel will co-occur with the messianic redemption of the people of Israel. This means that if humans themselves create

---

[36] On Muslim fundamentalism, see Tibi (2002). For helpful suggestions on fundamentalism in Islam, I thank Yaser Ellethy and Razi Quadir.

[37] As noted by Magid (2014a, 82).

a state of Israel, that counts as a defiance of God's will and probably only postpones the real redemption by the Messiah and the so-called ingathering of the exiles—that is, the return of the Jewish diaspora to the land of Israel.[38] That said, parts of modern Hasidism have developed more toward Rabbi Kook's Zionism (more on this shortly).

Orthodox responses to modernity like Habad and Satmar are deeply shaped by what has been called the "cultural ethos of religious freedom in America" (Magid 2014b, 103): they flourish due to the church-state division and the freedom to build one's own religious community, sometimes bordering on a parallel society. Things are, of course, different in Israel itself, where there may still be to some extent a parallel society, but the groups have clearly more institutionalized political clout. Here, Haredi fundamentalism takes a somewhat different shape. An example is the fundamentalist views of the Shas party, founded in 1984. The party is Sephardic and Mizrahi rather than Ashkenazi, the acronym meaning "Sephardic guardians of the Torah." The Shas party is characterized by purist ideology, rejection of gay and lesbian culture, strict adherence to Jewish law, separation between the sexes, xenophobia (for instance, toward Russian immigrants), and the inside/outside dichotomy between Jewish and non-Jewish people. It used to be fiercely opposed to Zionism, but that is no longer the case. As Nissim Leon (2014) has argued, this party has moved from the countersociety or parallel-society approach characteristic of many fundamentalisms to a more involved attitude regarding politics: it confers profound religious value on Jewish territory and Jewish nationalism.

Use of the term *fundamentalism* is the most contested for the third group—religious Zionism. Some think that we can properly use the term for this group (Leon 2014), whereas others claim this is misleading (e.g., Cahan 2014). Religious Zionism combines Orthodox Judaism with Zionism. Its members are also called *dati'im le'umim* (national religious). Crucial to the movement are the land of Israel (*eretz Israel*), the people of Israel, and the Torah. What Zionists themselves would qualify as early advocates, such as Yehuda Shlomo Alkalai and Zvi Hirsch Kalischer, already championed the return to Israel and the revival of everyday use of Hebrew. The main proponent in their view was Rabbi Abraham Isaac Kook (1865–1935), who provided a religious justification for the Zionist movement by arguing that it was a tool in God's hand to re-establish Jewish rule in Israel, the promised homeland of the Jewish people. Another well-known defender was the Lithuanian Rabbi Yitzchak Yaakov

---

[38] For a more detailed description of Habad and Satmar Hasidism, see Ravitzky (1996) and particularly Biale et al. (2018).

Reines (1839–1915), who founded the Mizrahi religious Zionist movement in 1902. In his works, he argued that the Zionist settlement of the land of Israel was unrelated to the future messianic redemption of the Jews and, therefore, did not constitute a heretical defiance of God's will. Contemporary religious Zionism is characterized by strong nationalism. It comprises such radical groups as Gush Emunim and the Kach party (banned for racism). Most religious Zionists support right-wing political parties. Many of the West Bank settlers are religious Zionists. Since it is so highly contested and many important properties charac-teristic of fundamentalism are missing, religious Zionism will not be included here as fundamentalist.

As previously indicated, what makes the other groups fundamentalist differs from movement to movement. For Haredi Judaism, it is the anti-modernism and strong anti-secularism in particular, men's control over women, and, closely related to that, strong patriarchal family structures. Furthermore, although, as I mentioned earlier, we do not find literalism about the Torah in Haredi Judaism, we do find strict adherence to *halakha* (Jewish law). This particular twitch to literalism is not surprising, since Judaism is more concerned with orthopraxis (right behavior) than with orthodoxy (right belief and right doctrine) anyway.

Now, how large are these groups in Judaism, which totals about 15 million people worldwide? The number of Hasidim is relatively small. The largest Hasidic group, the Satmar Hasidim, counts some 26,000 households, and Habad counts some 17,000 households. Still, given that these households comprise many family members, their total number is not negligible. The Haredi community is even larger. It is found primarily in Israel, and it is estimated it now constitutes about 13 percent of Israel's population, counting some 1.8 million people worldwide. In fact, given the high birth rate and the virtual absence of marriages with people from other faiths, it is growing rapidly. We can conclude, then, that there is a substantial minority of fundamentalists— probably somewhere between 15 and 20 percent—in Judaism. But this number may well grow over the coming years because, purely in demographic terms, Jewish fundamentalist movements are thriving, whereas birth rates are much lower among more-moderate Jews, particularly among liberal Jews.[39]

2.7 Fundamentalism in Hinduism

In the field of comparative fundamentalism studies, it is common to distinguish a distinct kind of Hindu fundamentalism. As Peter Huff (2008, 153) points out,

---

[39] For helpful suggestions here, I thank Daan Dijk, Jessica Roitman, and Bart Wallet. It struck me in writing this Element that there was more controversy on what to count as fundamentalist and what not when it came to Jewish fundamentalism than when it came to Christian or Islamic fundamentalism.

"Today when scholars refer to Hindu fundamentalism what they have in mind is an intentionally politicized Hinduism, dedicated to any number of the following values: defense of *Sanatana Dharma* (eternal religion); promotion of premodern gender roles; protection of a precisely defined confessional identity; and confrontation with Muslim, Christian, and secular opponents." Where did this come from, one may ask, and how does it manifest itself?

Let us start with the background. *Hinduism* is the name first used by Westerners for various religious faiths, ritual habits, and moral practices along the banks of the Indus and the Ganges, and in India in general.[40] The roots of Hinduism go back some 3,500 years. It is known for its diversity and inclusiveness, including toward local religious beliefs and practices. There are a few monotheistic strands in Hinduism, but it is largely radically polytheistic, acknowledging millions of gods. Over the last 100 years or so, Hinduism has seen a rapid rise of radical thought, fundamentalism, and nationalism, often denoted as Hindutva. Particularly since the Bharatiya Janata Party (BJP) was voted into power in May 2014, this Hindutva or Hindu fundamentalism has become a highly visible political phenomenon, even to such an extent that it is now common in the literature to speak of Hindu ethnonationalism. Sathianathan Clarke singles out three elements that he considers constitutive of such Hindu ethnonationalism or Hindu fundamentalism: "An idealized scriptural authority cultivated to unify the Hindu community; combative communal dispositions to form a social body that manifests the body of god; and the contradiction of violently *dualistic* religiopolitics based on *monistic* philosophy" (Clarke 2017, 96).

In the early twentieth century, some Hindus started to reach back to the past to reclaim what they thought of as a primordial Hindu essence, an essence that was suppressed by Muslim oppression, such as in certain stages of the Mughal occupation in the sixteenth and seventeenth centuries, but also by the British Empire during the era of Western colonialization. Thus, the quest began for a Hindu religious and political identity uncorrupted by "alien" Muslim and Christian colonial rule. Remarkably, much of this occurred in India in the 1920s, led by Vinayak Damodar Savarkar, around the same time Christian fundamentalism arose in the United States and the Muslim Brotherhood in Egypt. In his *Hindutva: Who Is a Hindu?*, published in 1923, Savarkar identifies what he considers to be the fundamentals of being a Hindu: utter devotion to the motherland, a blood connection with the Indian race going back to the Vedic fathers, and a common civilization, which has its roots in Brahmanism and is

---

[40] Hinduism, then, is as much a culture as it is a religion, as Chakrabarty and Jha (2020, 4) rightly point out.

contained in the Vedas, handed down in Sanskrit. In his understanding of Hindu identity, Christians and Muslims are vilified, while Hinduism becomes more muscular and militant. Savarkar's ideas were materialized by RSS, the National Volunteer Corps founded in 1925 by Keshav Baliram Hedgewar. RSS pursued a strong bodily culture of male fitness and was severely opposed to Muslim and Christian elements in India. It had 600,000 members in the early 1950s; today, it has more than 6 million members. In the 1980s, RSS experienced a revival and again began to influence India's politics, partly via other organizations it gave birth to, such as Vishva Hindu Parishad (VHP), founded by Madhav Sadashivrao Golwalkar and Shivram Shankar Apte, and the BJP, already mentioned here. Some think that the attempt to build India on a secular foundation,[41] as attempted by Jawaharlal Nehru and others, may have contributed to the rapid growth of these Hindu fundamentalist organizations.

In contemporary Hinduism, we find a narrative in terms of a perfect original state: the glorious rule and the military heroism of ancient Hindu culture as captured in *smriti* texts such as the epics of the Mahabharata and the Ramayana, Rama being the ideal king in the iconic city of Ayodhya. Then, the sacred territory of India, the Hindu body, was invaded by foreign rulers, Muslims and Christians in particular. And now, the ancient, perfect state of India for Hindus needs to be restored. To reach this aim, contemporary Hindu fundamentalists do not shy away from violence toward Muslims and Christians, including rape, murder, and the burning of churches and mosques.[42]

The BJP stated in 2015 that it has some 100 million members.[43] In February 2022, it became India's largest political party, one without a single Muslim representative. Clearly then, we are not talking about a negligible phenomenon but about fundamentalism becoming mainstream and influencing the lives of hundreds of millions of people out of the 1.2 billion Hindus worldwide. Even those who have hesitations about using the term *fundamentalism* here will have to acknowledge that discrimination on the basis of religion, culture, and race, nationalism, rejection of such parts of modernity as its liberal ethics, othering, legitimation of violence, idealization of the past, and other

---

[41] This attempt was at least partly successful: India's 1959 constitution is a secular document, which claims state neutrality toward all religions and "non-communalism" in the sense of making no appeal to religion-based identity in the public life of the nation-state (Ram-Prasad 2005, 532).

[42] Some figures in Hindu fundamentalism have argued that society needs to be ordered hierarchically, in correspondence with the four parts of the universal cosmic being. In the *varna* (caste) system based on professions, the *Brahmin* are parallel to his mouth, the *Kshatriyas* to his arms, the *Vaisyas* to his thighs, and the *Sudras* to his feet. Each caste comes with its own duties that should not be violated, because it is the embodiment of a part of the cosmic being. I have not included this as a characteristic, since others, including leading fundamentalist figures, reject this idea.

[43] This may be true, but it may also be propaganda—hard to say at this stage.

characteristics of fundamentalism and extremism are rampant in contemporary Indian Hinduism.[44] This is not to vilify Hindus or even to problematize Hinduism; it is simply to honestly and accurately describe a substantial segment of contemporary Hindus in order to show that fundamentalism is by no means unique to monotheistic religions.[45]

2.8 Market Fundamentalism

Arguably, secular fundamentalism comes in many shapes and sizes: radical environmentalism, left-wing extremism, neo-Nazism, Maoism and other kinds of communism, gender fundamentalism, scientific fundamentalism or scientism, market fundamentalism, and many more. Here, let us zoom in on market fundamentalism, a specific variety of secular fundamentalism that is also called free-market fundamentalism, economic fundamentalism, or capitalist fundamentalism.[46]

The term denotes a set of ideas and an approach to life in which the free market or economic laissez-faire is thought to be able to solve most economic and even social problems. The greatest wealth and well-being for the greatest number of people is produced when individuals are allowed to pursue their own financial interests without any kind of restraint or regulation.

Lee Boldeman, for instance, speaks of *market fundamentalism*—a term he prefers to *economic rationalism*, *market ideology*, and *free-market radicalism* because, on the one hand, it emphasizes the fundamentalist and what he considers religious nature of these "extreme beliefs," as he calls them, and because, on the other hand, it points to the source of these ideas, namely, an economic theory. Boldeman does not shy away from rather pejorative definitions of this phenomenon, such as "an uncritical and excessive adulation of markets."[47] Slightly more precisely and less pejoratively put, market fundamentalists have "a strong faith in unregulated markets and an associated distrust of governments, politics, politicians, government bureaucrats, government services and welfare provision." Such market fundamentalism often overlooks the pervasive influences that various kinds of power, wealth, and information asymmetries have and what they mean for people's incomes and prospects in society. Boldeman is somewhat unclear as to what exactly market fundamentalism

---

[44] That fundamentalism flourishes in Hinduism is also argued by Gierycz (2020). See also Nanda (2003); Fernandes (2007); Nussbaum (2007).

[45] For helpful suggestions regarding fundamentalism in Hinduism, I thank Clyde Missier and Victor Bijlert.

[46] Market fundamentalism has been described in detail by Kelsey (1995); Cox (2016).

[47] Boldeman (2007, Chapter 1). He describes the framework as "mainstream, dogmatic, mechanistic, imperialist, and fundamentalist" and deems it "naïve, simplistic ... economic theorizing," while he speaks of the policies that flow from it as "dehumanizing and stupid." Market fundamentalism is both an "idealization and an idolization of markets."

amounts to contentwise, but given what he argues against, it follows that he conceptualizes it as the collection of the following, related claims that jointly provide a framework for thinking about politics and social life as a whole:

- Economics can provide a convincing overarching theory of government action or social action more generally.
- Economics can define an ideal form of social or economic organization against which to measure our institutional and organizational arrangements.
- The invisible hand of the market will operate unaided to maximize individual and social welfare.
- Human welfare and happiness just *is* economic welfare.

An example he gives of such market fundamentalism is the view of John Stone, Australia's Secretary to the Treasury from 1979 to 1984, who claimed that "markets will, generally speaking and over time, always provide economically more advantageous outcomes than governments" (Stone 2000).[48]

Boldeman's choice for the word *fundamentalism* is far from accidental. He explicitly appeals to Marty and Appleby's influential *Fundamentalism Project* and speaks of "doctrinal simplicity," a "proselytizing nature," and a "special mission in the world sanctioned by God," as well as of "an exotic closed system of knowledge." In other words, he uses this term not merely because of its pejorative nature but because of what he considers to be structural similarities between, say, early twentieth-century reactionary American evangelicalism, on the one hand, and contemporary uncompromising faith in the market based on simplistic economic theory, on the other.

It is hard to come up with any well-based estimation of the number of market fundamentalists. Moreover, people who consider themselves affiliated with a particular religion can also embrace market fundamentalism. Yet, it is undeniable that there is, as such, nothing religious about market fundamentalism and that many who believe in it do not affiliate with a monotheistic religion or, in fact, with any religion at all. Again, then, we see that fundamentalism can also flourish beyond the boundaries of monotheism.

2.9 Conclusion

It is time to take stock. We have dispelled the myth—upheld by various influential authors in theology, philosophy, psychology, and religious studies—that fundamentalism is a specifically or typically monotheistic problem. True, some

---

[48] Other proponents of market fundamentalism, according to Boldeman, are Jack Hirshleifer and Gary Backer.

monotheistic believers have turned fundamentalist, sometimes even large groups of them. However, fundamentalism and related phenomena, such as violence, othering, and moral dualism, can equally be found in polytheistic religions, such as Hinduism, and in secular worldviews, such as market fundamentalism. We could easily add further examples: Sikh and Theravada nationalist Buddhist fundamentalism, left-wing extremism, certain kinds of ecofundamentalism, gender fundamentalism, and much more. Of course, this is not to deny that there may be elements—for instance, beliefs and practices—in monotheistic religions that fundamentalists can appeal to and use in expressing their motivations and formulating their goals. In Section 3, we turn to such beliefs and practices and explore whether, from a theological and philosophical point of view, there is something about their form or content that is conducive to fundamentalism.

3 Is Monotheistic Theology Conducive to Fundamentalism?

3.1 Introduction

The main question in this section is whether there is anything about the theologies of monotheism that leads to, encourages, or raises the likelihood of fundamentalism in general or religious fundamentalism in particular. This is possible even if, as we saw in the previous section, fundamentalism is not significantly more prevalent in monotheisms than in polytheisms or secular belief systems. After all, particular beliefs and practices in monotheisms may still steer individuals or groups in fundamentalist directions. We will consider various areas in which this might be the case: first and foremost, ideational and doctrinal areas, such as belief in absolute truth, the doctrine of God, soteriology, the theology of revelation, and the relation between faith and reason; and second, monotheisms' ethics and practical organizational characteristics.

One may worry whether the content of monotheisms truly factors into sound explanations of fundamentalism. Are these appeals to ideology, belief, or practice not post hoc rationalizations where accurate explanations would appeal to macrofactors like economic, social, and political circumstances? This is a complicated topic that deserves detailed attention of its own. But briefly, there is good empirical reason to think that extreme religious beliefs and practices of various kinds *do* partially explain extreme behavior.[49] This has been shown, for instance, for fundamentalism (see Brandt and Van Tongeren 2017, 76) and for terrorism (see De Graaf, forthcoming; De Graaf and Van den Bos 2021). It is, therefore, worthwhile to explore some representative beliefs and practices and ask whether they are conducive to fundamentalism.

---

[49] For more on what it is to explain, for example, extremism or fundamentalism, see Peels (2023c).

3.2 Belief in Absolute Truth

Many believers in the Abrahamic monotheisms believe in absolute truth—that is, truth that is universal and independent of the human mind. They believe in such truths as that God created the earth, that God is good, that God has revealed himself, and that humans are finite and sinful. This is certainly true for several official positions in these religions, such as Roman Catholic doctrine. Some of these truths are even thought to be necessary—for instance, the existence of God, the Trinity of God, and the moral goodness of praising God. One might think that this belief in absolute and objective truth is conducive to fundamentalism. After all, if there is objective, universal, mind-independent truth, then, given the diversity of religious and nonreligious views in this world, many are bound to be mistaken or at least to miss out on the truth. In fact, some scholars have included belief in universal truth among the characteristics of fundamentalism (e.g., Razaghi et al. 2020). Such belief in universal truth often comes with truth exclusivism—the idea that rival views must be false to the extent that they conflict with the core tenets of one's religious faith.[50]

Of course, belief in absolute truth and truth exclusivism can come with such cognitive vices as arrogance, epistemic insensitivity, epistemic oppression, and epistemic imperialism. But clearly, it does not need to do so; it can also come with great sympathy, interest in the person with whom one disagrees, and sincere dialogue. Furthermore, it is questionable that belief in absolute or universal truth is, as such, conducive to fundamentalism. First, there are all sorts of beliefs and belief systems widely accepted among nonfundamentalists that equally come with belief in absolute truth, such as the deliverances of logic, mathematics, and the natural sciences.[51] Moreover, many fully secular worldviews, such as various kinds of humanism, equally embrace belief in objective moral truth. In fact, most ethicists these days are moral realists, which means they believe in objective and mind-independent moral truth (see Bourget and Chalmers 2023). Finally, even those who reject exclusivism and defend pluralism are as a matter of fact themselves being exclusivist, because they claim that all parties are in some sense right and—whether or not they realize it—imply that exclusivism is wrong. A certain degree of exclusivism seems, therefore, inevitable, and it is not surprising then that monotheism usually comes with some degree of exclusivism. Second, belief in objective truth is just that: one believes there is an objective truth about God's existence or moral laws. Nothing

---

[50] Thus also Plantinga (2000b, 440). There is also soteriological or salvation-geared exclusivism and social exclusivism; I return to those later. For the distinction between these three kinds of exclusivism, see Grube (2023); Reitsma (2023).

[51] This is also pointed out by Gierycz (2020).

follows from that for how we should treat or think of those who do not believe in such truths. In other words, truth exclusivism does not imply social exclusivism. True, for people who are highly relativist about truth, so that all truth is just a matter of perspective and everybody is in a sense equally right (or equally wrong), it is quite hard to be a fundamentalist. But obviously, a movement is not fundamentalist just because its opposite rules out fundamentalism.

3.3 The Doctrine of God

Jonathan Kirsch has argued that the very idea that there is only one God inspires "ferocity" and "fanaticism." Polytheism is "open-minded" and has an "easygoing approach to religious belief and practice," whereas monotheism comes with "the sure conviction that only a single god exists, a tendency to regard one's own rituals and practices as the only proper way to worship the one true god" (Kirsch 2004, 2). Similarly, Ulrick Beck suggests that acknowledgment of the one and only true God implies cosmic dualism and the othering of those who do not believe in this God:

> The distinction between "we" and the "others" becomes emotionally charged by the cosmic struggle between the "powers of good" that have to overcome the "powers of evil" if the world is to be saved. In this way, the absolute nature of the one-and-only monotheistic God creates an entire world of "others" who have to be combated. Brutes and subhumans of every type—labels such as heretics, heathen, apostates, idolaters, renegades, etc., abound . . . —they are the flip side, the dark side, and the violent side with whose assistance universal Christianity conjures up a transethnic humanity. (Beck 2010, 54–5)

Are they right about the Abrahamic religions? Well, let us begin at the beginning: theology and doctrine are one thing and lived religion another, but by and large the Abrahamic religions can indeed rightly be considered monotheistic. Deuteronomy 6:4, which is the first part of the Shema, is often interpreted in this way. It says: "Hear, O Israel: The Lord our God, the Lord is one."[52] God tolerates no other gods besides him. In fact, this idea became so prominent during certain periods of ancient Judaism that God is described as jealous and that it is even said that his name is Jealous: "Do not worship any other god, for the Lord, whose name is Jealous, is a jealous God" (Exodus 34:14).[53] This idea is echoed throughout the history of Judaism. It is in a sense the core idea in this religion. Maimonides, for instance, formulates the second of his thirteen principles of the Jewish faith as follows: "He who is the cause of everything is One, not like the unity of a genus and not like the unity of a species; . . . rather, He,

---

[52] All Bible quotations are from the New International Version.
[53] For this alleged character trait of God and how to make sense of it, see Peels (2020).

may He be exalted, is One and His unity is such that there is no other unity like it in any manner" (Maimonides 1981, 151).

The idea that there is only one God remains pivotal in Christianity. Saint Paul, for instance, concludes at some point in his first letter to the Corinthians: "So then, about eating food sacrificed to idols: We know that 'An idol is nothing at all in the world' and that 'There is no God but one'" (1 Corinthians 8:4). Of course, Christianity's idea that God is triune complicates things. But official church doctrine is clear on this: even though there are three persons (Father, Son, and Holy Spirit), there is only one God or one being, having a single divine nature. For instance, the Nicene-Constantinopolitan Creed, formulated in 381, says:

> We believe in one God, the Father Almighty, Maker of heaven and earth, and of all things visible and invisible; and in one Lord Jesus Christ, the Son of God, the Only-begotten, Begotten of the Father before all ages, Light of Light, Very God of Very God, Begotten, not made; of one essence with the Father. ... And we believe in the Holy Spirit, the Lord, and Giver of Life, Who proceeds from the Father, Who with the Father and the Son together is worshipped and glorified.

Islam very much agrees with Judaism and Christianity when it comes to its unambiguous affirmation of God's oneness and calls it *tawhid*: the indivisible oneness of God. Numerous suras witness to this: "Worship Allah alone and associate none with Him" (Koran 4:36a). "Say, O Prophet, 'Come! Let me recite to you what your Lord has forbidden to you: do not associate others with Him in worship'" (Koran 6:151). "Do not set up any other god with Allah, or you will end up condemned, abandoned. For your Lord has decreed that you worship none but Him" (Koran 17:22–3). Sometimes, Islam's monotheism is explicitly contrasted with polytheism:

> The polytheists argue, "Had Allah willed, neither we nor our forefathers would have worshipped anything other than Him, nor prohibited anything without His command." So did those before them. Is not the messengers' duty only to deliver the message clearly? We surely sent a messenger to every community, saying, "Worship Allah and shun false gods." But some of them were guided by Allah, while others were destined to stray. So travel throughout the land and see the fate of the deniers! (Koran 16:35–6)

In fact, Islam even explicitly rejects Christian Trinitarianism: "Those who say, 'Allah is one in a Trinity,' have certainly fallen into disbelief. There is only One God. If they do not stop saying this, those who disbelieve among them will be afflicted with a painful punishment" (Koran 5:73).[54]

---

[54] All translations here are from Mustafa Khattab, *The Clear Quran*, as found at https://quran.com/. For more on Islam's monotheism, see Ibn Ṣaalih al-'Uthaymeen (1997); Dehlvi (2006).

It is hard to see how there is anything about the doctrine of the oneness of God as such that implies or renders likely some kind of fundamentalism. If there was, many polytheisms would equally be at risk. After all, many of them accept some kinds of gods but reject others. And atheism, of course, rules out the existence of any kind of god. It seems, then, that a worldview comes with a risk of fundamentalism only if it entails certain ideas about what this means for those who worship other gods or no gods whatsoever. We see the former at various junctures in the Tanakh, when religious believers are incited to use violence against those who worship idols, such as Baal and Asherah, the gods of the Canaanites (e.g., Numbers 25), or even to kill an entire people, children included (Deuteronomy 7). Naturally, the fact that it was allegedly God's command *in those circumstances, at that time, and at that place* does not imply that believers ought to display similar behavior now, but it is easy to see how such passages can be interpreted as justifying othering or even the use of violence. Such passages have bothered, and continue to deeply bother, Christian, Jewish, and Islamic theologians.

That said, there are other passages in these holy scriptures that advocate a radically different attitude, and in the case of Christianity especially, there is a salvation-historical dimension to this that renders unequivocal appeal to earlier passages problematic. Christians are called to turn the other cheek and love their enemies (Matthew 5:39, 44). They should bless those who persecute them, they should try to live in peace with everyone, they should not take revenge, they should feed their enemies, and they should overcome evil with good (Romans 12:14–21).

3.4 Soteriology

Another doctrinal area in which one might expect to find fertile soil for fundamentalism is soteriology—that is, the doctrine of salvation. Some religions and worldviews embrace the thought that there are multiple ways in which humans can be saved from their finite and sinful condition, but Abrahamic religions tend to be rather exclusive on this point. In other words, they display salvation-geared exclusivism.[55] Particularly poignant on this issue is Christianity, at least on its more orthodox interpretations. Jesus Christ himself, in John 14:6, claims: "I am the way and the truth and the life. No one comes to the Father except through me." The salvific work of Christ is the only road to redemption. Saint Paul, in his letter to the Philippians, weds eschatology to this exclusivist soteriology when he says: "Therefore God exalted him [Jesus] to the

---

[55] Thus also Grube (2023, 28), who also helpfully explains how truth-geared and salvation-geared exclusivism are conceptually related, yet distinct.

highest place and gave him the name that is above every name, that at the name of Jesus every knee should bow, in heaven and on earth and under the earth, and every tongue acknowledge that Jesus Christ is Lord, to the glory of God the Father" (Philippians 2:9–11).

This exclusive soteriology understandably also impacts missiology. After all, if there is only one way to be saved—namely, through Christ—and if God is the God of all humanity, then this news needs to reach all people. Consequently, some scholars see *evangelism* as a core characteristic of fundamentalism. According to James Deal and Karin Bartoszuk (2014, 266), for instance, "evangelism is an emphasis on reaching out to those individuals who are not saved, who are not a part of the church, with the goal of having them see and embrace the truth; this is the emphasis of preaching within the fundamentalist church, with a number of other outreach venues used, as well." They are surely right that evangelism is a core characteristic of early twentieth-century evangelical fundamentalism; this has been shown in detail by, among others, George Marsden (1980). The approach of the early twentieth-century fundamentalists also shows the wedding of evangelism with eschatology. It was common for them, for instance, to speak of what they called the "blessed hope," the imminent premillennial return of Christ to earth (Watt 2014, 21).

In the philosophy of religion, there is a long-standing debate on the status of such exclusivism. Leading figures such as John Hick have rejected it as being morally or epistemically deficient, while others, such as Alvin Plantinga, have argued that there is nothing epistemically or morally objectionable about it and that we are exclusivist about many other issues in life, including ones that are not directly related to religion (see, e.g., Hick 2004, 235; Plantinga 2000a). We find a somewhat similar debate in Judaism. In his book *The Dignity of Difference* (2002), for example, Chief Rabbi Jonathan Sacks argues that no religion, Judaism included, has a monopoly on spiritual truth and that wisdom, knowledge, righteousness, and even a true relationship with God can be found in all religions. In response to criticisms from various orthodox rabbis, such as Yosef Shalom Elyashiv and Bezalel Rakow, he felt compelled to revise the book on a couple of issues.

Soteriological exclusivism can be and has indeed been appealed to and used in justifying certain fundamentalist beliefs and practices. However, there is nothing about such religious exclusivism as such that steers one in the direction of fundamentalism. On the one hand, mainstream nonfundamentalist monotheistic religions often equally embrace religious exclusivism. Take the opening sentences of the Athanasian Creed, which is formally accepted by the Roman Catholic Church, the Eastern Church, and various Lutheran, Reformed, and Anglican churches:

> Whosoever will be saved (*quicumque vult salvus esse*), before all things it is
> necessary that he hold the catholic faith. Which faith unless every one do keep
> whole and undefiled, without doubt he shall perish everlastingly (*in aeternum
> peribit*). And the catholic faith is this: that we worship one God in Trinity, and
> Trinity in Unity; neither confounding the Persons, nor dividing the Essence. For
> there is one Person of the Father; another of the Son; and another of the Holy
> Ghost.

The creed was formulated to criticize the heresy of Arianism[56] and further
elaborate the Trinitarian theology of the First Councils of Nicaea (held in 325)
and Constantinople (held in 381)—hence the focus on Christology—but this
time, it is framed soteriologically. In church life, of course, things are more
complicated; few would claim that having faith in God or even having belief in
God is incompatible with having doubts. But the very fact that this creed is part
of church doctrine questions the idea that soteriological exclusivism as such
distinguishes fundamentalism from mainstream religion.

On the other hand, more-immanent but equally exclusivist salvation theories
can be found in more-secular worldviews, such as humanism and Marxism. For
instance, in classical Marxism, which is radically materialist, the basic idea is
that we can improve our political institutions, legal systems, social relations,
and aesthetic way of life by revising how society is economically organized, or,
more specifically, by altering its mode of production. Karl Marx, Friedrich
Engels, and others argue that as technology improves, various modes of production become obsolete. The socialist solution classical Marxists propose
comprises such things as cooperative ownership rather than private property,
production for general human needs rather than for private benefit, the abolition
of classes (particularly the annulment of the divide between the proletariat and
the bourgeoisie), and if necessary—some argue it is inevitable—a socialist
revolution in which the lower classes seize the state so as to avoid exploitation
by higher classes and in which capitalism is overthrown.[57] This materialist and
fully immanent framework takes it that this far-reaching economic and social
reorganization is the *only* solution to the problem and the only route to a society
in which all human beings flourish. Alternative economic models, such as
feudal systems and capitalism in particular, are thought to be doomed.
Exclusivism, then, is by no means unique to monotheistic religion, not even
to religion generally.[58]

---

[56] Arianism is the theology that says that Jesus Christ—or the Son of God, the Logos—was
a creature begotten by God with a substance similar to that of the Father, but not identical to God.

[57] For an introduction to the original ideas, see Marx (1859); Engels (1880). For a contemporary
exploration of classical Marxism in more detail, see Hudis et al. (2018).

[58] I particularly thank Dirk-Martin Grube for helpful comments on Section 3.4.

3.5 Doctrine of Scripture

We saw that a core characteristic of fundamentalism is the way it seeks to formulate indubitable fundamentals. In the case of monotheistic fundamentalisms, such principles are often generated by a literal-historical reading of relevant holy scriptures. Paul Williamson, for instance, has argued with others that fundamentalists' attitudes to sacred texts have six dimensions (see Williamson et al. 2010). The text is taken to be

1. *divine*: the text is of divine origin rather than the product of a human mind; it is a revelation to all humanity;
2. *inerrant*: the text is objectively true and contains no errors, contradictions, or inconsistencies; potential inconsistencies are always reconciled;
3. *self-interpretative*: the text is enough for understanding the divine intention; we do not need outside sources, like scholarly criticism or archeology;
4. *privileged*: the text stands above all other texts;[59]
5. *authoritative*: the text is the final authority, superior to any other texts;
6. *unchanging*: the text is immutable and timeless; it always tells us how life ought to be understood and lived, no matter how the times change.

Monotheistic religions differ in the extent to which they embrace, reject, or qualify claims along these lines. That has to do with such things as their theory of revelation: whereas most Christians would accept a so-called *organic theory* of revelation, on which the writing of these sacred texts was a matter of a complex interaction between the Holy Spirit and humans with all their talents and deficiencies, most Muslims would embrace a more *mechanistic theory* of revelation, on which the prophet Muhammad, who was said to be illiterate, orally shared the words of Allah with his followers, who would then write them down verbatim. Even in Islam, though, not all of these six properties are usually ascribed to the Koran or the Hadith. It is widely believed, for instance, that scholarly criticism and interpretation are needed to better understand these holy writings.

Moreover, at least two core characteristics of how Abrahamic fundamentalists usually treat their holy scriptures seem to be missing from Williamson's list. These characteristics involve

7. *literalism*: the text is meant to be read literally and historically in its entirety;
8. *epistemic exclusivism*: the text is the only relevant source of knowledge in the sense that religious mystical experience, tradition, common sense, and the like cannot teach us anything about the divine.

---

[59] In other words, it stands on a higher footing. What this presumably means is that in the case of conflict, the sacred text always trumps other texts.

Literalism is a core characteristic of fundamentalism and one of the things that distinguish fundamentalism from mainstream religion. In mainstream Judaism, Christianity, and Islam, it is acknowledged that there are different genres in the holy scriptures: they contain historical passages but also poems, songs, epistles, fables, riddles, prophecies, chokmatic or wisdom writings, laws, and apocalyptic passages—each with their own hermeneutical standards. There are literal but also allegorical, tropological, analogical, typological, and many other kinds of readings, and sometimes multiple readings can be equally valid.[60]

The eighth characteristic, epistemic exclusivism, also distinguishes the fundamentalist approach to holy texts from the approach of mainstream religions: the latter acknowledge a wide variety of sources, even about the divine, beyond those texts, such as personal religious experience, tradition, common sense, reason, and in some cases even other religions. Abrahamic fundamentalisms often exclude such sources. As Simon Wood (2014, 134) points out, for instance, "fundamentalism is known for hostility toward mysticism."

Therefore, even though fundamentalist readings of holy scripture may share certain characteristics with conservative readings or even mainstream readings, they are also clearly distinct from the hermeneutics of mainstream Abrahamic religions.

3.6 Faith and Reason

Religions have different views on how faith and reason relate to one another, and one can even find drastically different ideas on this within particular religions, monotheistic ones included. A couple of authors have argued that what distinguishes religions and worldviews that are fertile soil for fundamentalism from those that are not is their conceptualization of the relation between faith and reason. Says Michał Gierycz (2020, 11):

> A hypothesis may be proposed that fertile soil for fundamentalism may be provided by religions which not only claim to carry a universal truth (which is a constitutive element of nearly all religions as well as secular convictions concerning outlook), but which do not necessarily link it with the order of reason, or which are irrational by their very nature, and so, as pointed out by Gilles Kepel . . . , eluding the logic of reason. A doctrine more open to the *ratio*, in light of this hypothesis, would be less susceptible to becoming a soil for the "fundamentalist mindset" than a doctrine which says that the will of God or gods is not related to the category of rationality.

---

[60] In fact, this has been the dominant position in, for instance, the church for most of its history, as Sarot (2011, 253–4) points out. Sarot also shows how literalism and infallibilism have their roots in certain kinds of seventeenth-, eighteenth-, and nineteenth-century theologies (e.g., the work of Francis Turretin and, later, A. A. Hodge).

Note that Gierycz here speaks of the "fundamentalist mindset." But what is this supposed to be, and is there even such a thing? Many authors have stated there is indeed a fundamentalist mindset, but they differ in what they claim such a mindset amounts to: irrationality and unreasonableness; thinking styles, such as paranoia or dualistic thinking; apocalyptic thinking; certain epistemic relations to charismatic leadership; and cognitive vices, like dogmatism, narrow-mindedness, and credulity.[61]

Gierycz makes his point in terms of the relation between the will of God and rationality. At the background here is the famous voluntarism-rationalism debate. Already in Plato's *Euthyphro*, we find the question of whether something is good because God wills it or whether God wills something because it is good. Roughly, voluntarists claim that something is good because God wills it—*voluntas* meaning "will"—whereas rationalists argue either that God wills something because it is good or that this is somehow a false dilemma. Rationalists are more inclined to trust our moral reasoning because it gives us insight into moral truth, and God will inevitably believe moral truth. And, of course, this reflects on how we should live: we should follow human reason. An example would be Pope Benedict XVI's (2006) approach when he said: "Not to act in accordance with reason is contrary to God's nature."[62] Rationalists generally believe in such things as common grace and general revelation both about God and about morality, for instance, as described in Romans 1 and 2. Many of them are rather sympathetic, then, toward natural theology, which seeks to argue for God's existence and moral truths on the basis of generally accessible grounds. According to voluntarists, on the other hand, something becomes good because God wills it (divine command theory), and our moral intuitions may thus often not be a reliable guide for finding moral truth. We should rather rely on holy scriptures in which God communicates moral laws to us, such as the Decalogue (Exodus 20 and Deuteronomy 5) and the Sermon on the Mount (Matthew 5–7).

Gierycz (2020, 13) has argued that Islam is thoroughly voluntarist and that the same holds for Hinduism, with its contradictory beliefs about God or the divine. He concludes that "the fundamentalist potential of Islam or Hinduism is profoundly higher than that of Christianity, and of Catholicism in particular" (2020, 13).

How should we think of this suggestion? It may well be true that fundamentalism is somewhat more prominent in denominations or churches in which voluntarism is more widely accepted—we already saw that it is more prominent in Protestantism than in Roman Catholicism. Yet, that may have numerous other

---

[61] For many of these, see Strozier et al. (2010).

[62] In saying this, he was summarizing and approvingly quoting the alleged words of the Byzantine emperor Manuel II Palaiologos.

reasons, having to do with the role of scripture, the relation to tradition, and the role of ecclesiastic hierarchy in exegetical authority—things to which we return later. Not just anything that correlates with fundamentalism is explanatorily relevant.

Moreover, some churches are primarily voluntarist—and nominalist—while knowing little fundamentalism. An example would be the Lutheran Church. Luther, following Ockham, defended a radically voluntarist conception of God and was highly dismissive of any attempt of reason to probe into the nature of God or the truths of morality. Furthermore, there seems to be a bit of a mismatch between the explanans and the explanandum. If the idea is that in churches where voluntarism is the majority position, people take it that God can command just anything and that they can therefore not rely on their own moral intuitions when God allegedly asks them to do something intuitively immoral, then that would explain at most immoral action, such as violent extremism in general or maybe even terrorism in particular. But that is a far cry from fundamentalism, which, as we saw, is constituted by such stereotypical properties as the search for certainty, anti-modern sentiments, and a particular kind of narrative in terms of paradise, fall, and restoration.

In monotheistic religions, we also find branches that disconnect faith from reason and sometimes even present them as opposed to one another. This approach is called *fideism*—from the Latin *fides*, which means "faith." The core idea is that we should forego rational inquiry and rely on faith alone. Exactly whose theology counts as fideist is controversial in quite a few cases, but in Christianity, figures often associated with it—whether rightly or wrongly so[63]—are Tertullian, Blaise Pascal, Søren Kierkegaard, William James, and Ludwig Wittgenstein.[64]

One might think that immunity to rational questioning increases the chances of taking a fundamentalist turn, because othering, animosity, moral dualism, and the like can no longer be questioned by reason. In reply, we should first note that fideism, in Christianity, for instance, has always been a minority position: the vast majority of theologians and churches has embraced the value of reason in faith and has sought to reconcile religion with science and other kinds of rational inquiry. Second and even more importantly, it is specifically *fides*—that is, one's faith in God—that in fideism is disconnected from reason. It does not follow that one's morality, the rules and regulations of one's community, one's relation to culture, and so on, cannot be questioned by reason.

---

[63] For what it's worth: I think Tertullian, Blaise Pascal, and William James are wrongly classified as fideists. Only Kierkegaard and Wittgenstein are serious candidates here.

[64] For more on this, see Amesbury (2022).

3.7 Thorny Texts

Now that we have seen that there is little in the beliefs, practices, and organizational structures of the Abrahamic religions that would be conducive to fundamentalism, let me stress that there are numerous passages in the holy scriptures of the Tanakh, the Bible, and the Koran that, particularly on a literal-historical reading that takes the text to be infallible, can easily be interpreted as supportive of fundamentalism. To show this, let us consider some texts from each of them.

The first is a passage from a long speech by Moses in which he retells the national epic. The opening verses of Deuteronomy 7 sketch how God commands to exterminate the native people of Canaan:

> When the Lord your God brings you into the land you are entering to possess and drives out before you many nations—the Hittites, Girgashites, Amorites, Canaanites, Perizzites, Hivites and Jebusites, seven nations larger and stronger than you—and when the Lord your God has delivered them over to you and you have defeated them, then you must destroy them totally. Make no treaty with them, and show them no mercy. Do not intermarry with them. Do not give your daughters to their sons or take their daughters for your sons, for they will turn your children away from following me to serve other gods, and the Lord's anger will burn against you and will quickly destroy you. (Deuteronomy 7:1–4)

Of course, this text is paradoxical from the very start: Why command the Jewish audience not to marry the Canaanites if they are meant to fully exterminate them in the first place? But more importantly for our purposes, to say that this passage concerns othering is an understatement: prima facie, the text seems to encourage enclave formation or even straightforwardly to demonize the other and to cultivate hatred and murder.[65] This text is, unfortunately, not unique in the Tanakh: Moses orders the killing of all Midianite men, boys, and women who have never slept with a man (Numbers 31:17–18), the prophet Samuel is allegedly sharing God's command when he orders the Israelites to kill all Amalekite men and women, children and infants, even cattle and sheep, camels and donkeys (1 Samuel 15:3), and the prophet Elijah orders the slaughter of hundreds of Baal's prophets (1 Kings 18:40). Even God himself is called a "warrior" (Exodus 15:3).

Turning to the Second Testament, we find passages that seem to testify of moral dualism and black-and-white thinking in the ethical realm, as if there is only good and evil, nothing in between, no nuance and no shades of grey, no

---

[65] For an analysis of the narrative in Deuteronomy 6 and 7 and how it sustains particular emotions of love, fear, and disgust, see Feldt (2023).

room for disagreement or compromise. Take what Jesus Christ himself says in Matthew 12:

> Whoever is not with me is against me, and whoever does not gather with me scatters. And so I tell you, every kind of sin and slander can be forgiven, but blasphemy against the Spirit will not be forgiven. Anyone who speaks a word against the Son of Man will be forgiven, but anyone who speaks against the Holy Spirit will not be forgiven, either in this age or in the age to come. (Matthew 12:30–2)

Not only does Christ seem to divide people and to suggest that all those who do not follow him are equally on the evil side, he also seems to claim that certain sins cannot be forgiven—a harsh statement that has led numerous people to deep depression and utter despair.

Or take what the author of 1 Timothy—possibly the apostle Paul—wrote about the role and place of women in relation to their husbands:

> A woman should learn in quietness and full submission. I do not permit a woman to teach or to assume authority over a man; she must be quiet. For Adam was formed first, then Eve. And Adam was not the one deceived; it was the woman who was deceived and became a sinner. But women will be saved through childbearing—if they continue in faith, love and holiness with propriety. (1 Timothy 2:11–15)

This is not exactly woke. In fact, it seems misogynous: it subjugates women and reduces their value to traditional gender roles such as childbirth, in passing blaming them—and partially exculpating men—for human evil.

Finally, an example from the Koran, the well-known "sword verse":

> But once the Sacred Months have passed, kill the polytheists who violated their treaties wherever you find them, capture them, besiege them, and lie in wait for them on every way. But if they repent, perform prayers, and pay alms-tax, then set them free. Indeed, Allah is All-Forgiving, Most Merciful. (Koran 9:5)

This text seems to leave little ambiguity: once the sacred months are over, pagans, nonbelievers, polytheists, and the like are free game for Muslims: unless they repent, one can simply slay them—another case of what seems plain hatred and aggression. Further texts that seem to commend animosity or straightforward violence can be found elsewhere in the Koran (e.g., Koran 2:191, 4:89, 8:39). An example that does not seem to involve an appeal to violence but nonetheless involves some sort of othering concerns so-called *al-walā' w' al-barā'* texts in the Koran, literally "loyalty and disavowal." These are texts saying that one should stay close to one's fellow believers and dissociate oneself from unbelievers. For instance:

Believers should not take disbelievers as guardians [sometimes translated as "helpers" or "friends"] instead of the believers—and whoever does so will have nothing to hope for from Allah—unless it is a precaution against their tyranny. And Allah warns you about Himself. And to Allah is the final return. (Koran 3:28)

This recommendation or command, taken at face value, only seems to enhance enmity and antagonism between Muslims and nonbelievers, and such texts are ubiquitous in the Koran (e.g., Koran 3:118–19, 4:144, 5:51, 5:57, 8:72, 8:73, 9:23, 60:1).

Now, these texts, more so than any doctrines or practices, have been conducive to fundamentalism—that is, when combined with a modern literal-historical reading that assumes the text is infallible, such as the kind of reading we find with the Muslim Brotherhood's leading figure Sayyid Qutb. For it is hard to deny that if these passages are read in this way, particularly when they are also read in isolation, they do indeed lend support to various stereotypical properties of fundamentalism, such as conservative gender roles and othering—and in fact in some cases to violent extremism.

Needless to say, these texts have been the object of detailed exegetical, hermeneutical, moral, and systematic-theological reflection and debate within these religions for centuries, in some cases even millennia. Mainstream Judaism, Christianity, and Islam have largely developed nuanced, often nonliteral, or historically situated and culturally contextualized readings of these passages. Exegetes have also time and again stressed that texts should be interpreted in light of other texts. For instance, *al-walā' w' al-barā'* texts in the Koran should be read in light of other verses, such as Koran 60:8, which encourages Muslims to treat kindly all just people, independently of their faith.[66]

Despite all of this, a few of these texts remain stumbling blocks to religious believers in these traditions themselves, even upon highly contextualized readings. However, they are then often thought to be outweighed by other texts that are believed to be more important and quantitively more prevalent and that call for peace, forgiveness, empathy, equality, and love. Here we can think of the following commandment in the Torah: "When a foreigner resides among you in your land, do not mistreat them. The foreigner residing among you must be treated as your native-born. Love them as yourself, for you were foreigners in Egypt. I am the Lord your God" (Leviticus 19:33–4). An example from the Second Testament is Jesus Christ's Sermon on the Mount (Matthew 5–7), which calls for turning the other cheek and blesses the meek and the peacemakers. In

---

[66] For a lucid and contextual reading of the *al-walā' w' al-barā'* texts, see Ellethy (2023). He also argues that this passage is often misunderstood and that it is perfectly compatible with a transreligious bond in which Muslims and non-Muslims share sociopolitical values.

the Koran, we find texts such as this: "Let there be no compulsion in religion, for the truth stands out clearly from falsehood" (Koran 2:256). The list is endless. Of course, no matter how long that list is, fundamentalists can always isolate particular texts and pursue a literal-historical reading that takes the text to be infallible, sometimes with dire epistemic and moral ramifications. Yet, since there are so many passages that clearly conflict with the thorny texts upon a literal-historical reading of the latter, we have good reason to think that even if one's holy scripture is divinely inspired, it should not be read literally in its entirety.

3.8 Conclusion

In this section, we had to be selective. We have considered only a few beliefs and practices from monotheistic religions that might be thought to be conducive to fundamentalism. The ones we did consider, however, seemed important candidates. It turned out that, even though they can be used—and have been used—to justify fundamentalism, there is nothing about them as such that steers one in that direction. What can lend support, though, to fundamentalism in the Abrahamic monotheisms are particular texts from the Tanakh, the Bible, and the Koran, particularly when such holy scripture is read in its entirety in a literal-historical manner that assumes the text is infallible.

4 Does Monotheism Have Resources for Resilience Toward Fundamentalism?

4.1 Introduction

So far, we have seen there is no empirical evidence to think that a positive correlation of any kind holds between monotheism and fundamentalism. More theoretically, that is, on a doctrinal level, we have seen there is nothing about monotheism's theologies that steers its believers in fundamentalist directions, even though some people evidently can and do use its texts and even its theologies for such purposes. In this final section, we explore an often-overlooked issue, namely, whether monotheisms provide resources for resilience toward fundamentalism—whether that be their doctrines, their practices, or their organizational structures. Rather than trying to be exhaustive, I use a couple of examples to show that monotheisms have plenty of capital to make individuals and groups more resilient toward fundamentalism.

This is not to say that there is no capital in other religions or worldviews to counter fundamentalism or that there are no public nonreligious resources to counter fundamentalisms in Abrahamic monotheisms. All this is undoubtedly true, but the focus here is on what monotheisms themselves have to offer in terms of resources to counter or deal with fundamentalism. Furthermore, fundamentalisms are not morally or epistemically problematic in every regard. Motivated by their fundamentalist views, values, and identity, fundamentalists have found personal meaning and solace, they have hidden Jewish people during World War II, they have displayed an exemplary work ethics, they have engaged in valuable scholarship, they have done great works of charity, and much more. However, it seems hard to deny that the unqualified dismissal of various branches of science, rejection of the rights of sexual minorities, denial of education to women, moral dualism, and othering are harmful, often both epistemically and morally. When we explore the resilience potential of monotheisms, then, we mean the potential to provide resilience toward these epistemically and morally detrimental dimensions of fundamentalism.

One may wonder how fundamentalisms can grow and flourish in certain monotheisms if there are tenets within those monotheisms that go against them. Yet, as Sathianathan Clarke (2017, 95) notes, "religions brazenly contradict even those beliefs most central to their identity," by which he presumably means that *movements within religions* can contradict beliefs central to those religions. In fact, humans can live with quite a bit of cognitive dissonance. This straightaway calls for realism: if it is possible for fundamentalist movements to contradict beliefs and practices that are central to the religious faith they belong to, then identifying those core beliefs and practices is, as such, no panacea guaranteed to make a community fully resistant to fundamentalism. It is probably wiser to think of such beliefs and practices merely as somewhat lowering the chances of fundamentalism or at least mitigating its consequences, as well as creating more resilience in religions toward fundamentalist thought and action.

This does not mean that such resilience fully prevents fundamentalism from occurring in the relevant religious community. That would be too demanding: virtually all religions and worldviews have had to deal at some point with fundamentalist developments within some of their subgroups. The notion of resilience, often used in contexts of developing counterextremism and counterterrorism strategies, concerns *whether* and *how* communities can bounce back from terrorist attacks and extremist actions. A recent example is Michelle Grossman and others' cross-cultural community-level BRAVE (Building Resilience Against Violent Extremism) measure, based on semistructured interviews in Canada and Australia meant to measure resilience toward violent extremism. Their twenty-item list contains such things as "engagement with diverse others" and "belief in nonviolent resolutions." Grossman and her co-authors define *resilience* as the ability to resist and challenge the social legitimation of violent extremist propaganda, recruitment and ideology as a response to social and political grievances, based on access to and capacity to navigate and mobilize socio-cultural resources for coping and thriving under adversity. (Grossman et al. 2022, 471)

We should, of course, carefully distinguish violent extremism from fundamentalism, but their notion of resilience is useful in the context of fundamentalism as well. Also, they speak of "socio-cultural" resources, so let me stress that no matter exactly how these are understood, such resources should also include *religious* resources. For our purposes, then, we can define *resilience* as the ability to resist and challenge the social legitimation of fundamentalist propaganda, recruitment, and ideology as a response to grievances, particularly toward modern developments, based on access to and capacity to navigate and mobilize sociocultural-religious resources for coping and thriving in the presence of fundamentalist challenges.

We should further note that high resilience in a particular religion or community does not imply low risk: the risks may be high, say, just because there is much fundamentalist discourse in a particular region or on a particular platform. Yet the community may be highly resilient in that it has resources to deal with and bounce back in the face of fundamentalism (Grossman et al. 2022, 469). Thus, we will here explore whether monotheisms have the resources not only to prevent fundamentalism but also to veer back, to adapt, and to transform[67] once some of their members or subcommunities turn fundamentalist. What are the protective capacities and community assets that monotheism can provide? What is the religious resilience capital that monotheistic religions themselves have?[68]

This question has often been overlooked. Maybe that is because of a secular bias and unfamiliarity with religion among many who study fundamentalism.[69] Maybe it is because of the widespread militant rhetoric against religion quite common among intellectuals nowadays. We live in a world in which Nobel Prize laureate Steven Weinberg can publicly say that "religion is an insult to human dignity. With or without religion, you would have good people doing good things and evil people doing evil things. But for good people to do evil things, that takes

---

[67] On the idea that resilience concerns not just veering back but also adapting and transforming, see Grossman (2021).

[68] This squares well with an approach to fundamentalism and extremism I am developing elsewhere in much more detail and which takes a first-person perspective: How can fundamentalism and extremism best be understood and explained, given what these actors themselves have got to say on what they believe and why they act as they do? See Peels (forthcoming).

[69] For the point about secular bias, see Dawson (2021a, 2021b).

religion"[70] and public debater Richard Dawkins can confidently say: "I think a case can be made that faith is one of the world's great evils, comparable to the smallpox virus but harder to eradicate."[71]

Fortunately, it is not entirely uncommon to think that monotheisms may have resources for resisting fundamentalism.[72] In an interview, R. Scott Appleby and Martin Marty, leaders of the seminal *Fundamentalism Project* (Marty and Appleby 1991–5), point out:

> To gain support beyond small cadres of followers, fundamentalist leaders must persuade ordinary believers to suspend existing teachings that condemn violence and promote peacemaking. Believers who are theologically informed and spiritually well formed tend not to be susceptible to such arguments. Unfortunately, ordinary believers are not always sufficiently grounded in the teachings and practices of their traditions to counter fundamentalists' selective reading of sacred texts. (Appleby and Marty 2009)

The idea here is that sufficient acquaintance with the "teaching and practices" of mainstream monotheistic religions will defeat or decrease susceptibility toward fundamentalism. But what exactly could these teachings and practices be, and how would they enable communities to bounce back in the face of fundamentalist challenges? Rather than trying to be exhaustive, I will elaborate on a couple of examples from doctrine and practice, particularly in Christianity and Judaism, to show what kinds of resources monotheisms may have for resilience.

4.2 The Image of God in Jewish, Christian, and Islamic Anthropology

A fundamental doctrinal idea in Jewish and Christian anthropology is that humans have been created in the image of God. This notion is based on such texts as Genesis 1:27, which reads: "So God created mankind in his own image (*tzelem elohim*), in the image of God he created them; male and female he created them." Exactly what this image of God (*imago Dei* in Christianity) is thought to amount to varies from one person's theology to that of another. Theologians like Augustine, Aquinas, and Maimonides embrace a *substantive* view: they believe it means that humans share characteristics with God. Others,

---

[70] Steven Weinberg in an address at the Conference on Cosmic Design, American Association for the Advancement of Science, Washington, DC, April 1999.

[71] Richard Dawkins in a speech in acceptance of the Humanist of the Year award of the American Humanist Association (AHA), 1996. It is worth emphasizing that most academics hold a much more favorable view about religion, as Elaine Ecklund and David Johnson have demonstrated in detail (Ecklund and Johnson 2021).

[72] Thus also Machasin (2009, 225), who argues that forms of religiosity that promote dialogue ought to be encouraged.

such as Karl Barth, Emil Brunner, and Benedict XVI, offer a *relational* view: they believe it is a matter of being related to God and one another. Yet others, such as Martin Luther, accept a *functional* view: they believe it means that humans have a particular function, such as representing God and being responsible for creation. We also find views of the *imago Dei* in terms of rationality, free will, being male and female, consciousness, the ability to speak, the ability to create and maintain complex relationships, and the ability to govern the earth.[73] Yet, what is common to all of them is that this image of God is not restricted to any country, race, gender, or even religion. Of course, some theologies add that this image of God has been severely damaged by sin, but again, there is no difference here across ethnicity, gender, or religion. Othering and creating sharp in-group/out-group boundaries can become much harder if one takes seriously the idea that all human beings have tremendous value because they are created in the image of God.

In the Second Testament, the notion is further developed in a way that makes Christian anthropology and soteriology meet: the idea is that Christ himself is the perfect image of God (e.g., Hebrews 1:3). That means that anyone who is in Christ and is thereby saved by Christ—any Christian, any follower of Christ—partakes in the perfect image of God. And that has consequences: "There is neither Jew nor Gentile, neither slave nor free, nor is there male and female, for you are all one in Christ Jesus" (Galatians 3:28). While this idea of being united in Christ naturally only holds for fellow Christians, it implies at least that, contrary to what we find in many Christian fundamentalist movements, there can be no othering of other Christians, say, because they are not strict enough or because they are female. Of course, one can add further ideas to this, such as that Christians beyond one's fundamentalist movement are not *true* Christians—for example, because they are too liberal. To say that an idea can provide resilience does not mean, then, that it cannot be suppressed by adding further ideas. Still, doing so will increase the chances of cognitive dissonance.

In Islam, the idea that humans are created in the image of God is more contested (Melchert 2011). Creation narratives in the Koran do not refer to an alleged image of God. However, human distinctness and, in a way, sanctity are confirmed by such things as the fact that Adam teaches the angels the names of all things and the fact that God commands the angels to prostrate before Adam (Koran 2:31–4). Some Islamic theologians, such as Ibn al-'Arabī, have gone further and argued that Adam had knowledge not so much of the names of all things as of all the names of God. Humans can respond to their creation by exemplifying the same attributes and virtues as God, such as forgiving the

---

[73] For an overview, see Middleton (2005).

unforgivable. Beyond the Koran, there are various words of the prophet Muhammad that have been interpreted as referring to the image of God. The first one is this: "God created Adam according to his *ṣūra*," but it is contested to whom "his" refers. There is no such syntactical ambiguity in another narration: "Verily, God created Adam according to the *ṣūra* of the Most Merciful." Here, however, its integrity has been contested (Çelik 2023).

Historically, the notion of human beings being created *imago Dei* has played a crucial role in debates on human rights and the dignity of human life, both in Christianity and in Judaism. In Genesis 9 already, for instance, the notion is a ground for the prohibition of murder. Ever since the early Puritans, the notion has been appealed to in formulating and defending human rights, at least in Anglo-Saxon contexts (not so much in the French context). The concept was also used in defending freedom of religion and in laying out our responsibility for the earth and for future generations—in Jürgen Moltmann's work, for example.

Theological ideas about the *imago Dei*, then, provide a resource for countering othering, for opposing all too strict a boundary between in-group and out-group, for rejecting violence against others, and for affirming the rights of people of other faiths and ethnicities. Thus, this notion offers important religious capital for building resilience toward fundamentalism.

4.3 Hermeneutics

Fundamentalisms, we saw, are *modern* phenomena. It is, therefore, unsurprising that the specifically modern characteristics of fundamentalism, such as a literal-historical reading of most Bible passages, do not find any support in these holy scriptures. But something stronger can be said: these holy scriptures themselves already employ hermeneutics that contradict a literal-historical reading across the board and therefore conflict directly with how fundamentalists read them. Take what the apostle Paul writes in Galatians 4:22–7:

> For it is written that Abraham had two sons, one by the slave woman and the other by the free woman. His son by the slave woman was born according to the flesh, but his son by the free woman was born as the result of a divine promise. These things are being taken figuratively: The women represent two covenants. One covenant is from Mount Sinai and bears children who are to be slaves: This is Hagar. Now Hagar stands for Mount Sinai in Arabia and corresponds to the present city of Jerusalem, because she is in slavery with her children. But the Jerusalem that is above is free, and she is our mother.

Paul's reading of the narrative of Genesis 16 is clearly *allegorical* rather than *literal-historical*. Typological readings, such as in Matthew 1:23 and 1 Corinthians 15:22, are another example of nonliteral-historical readings in the Second

Testament. The idea that the entirety of the Bible is meant to be read literally and historically is highly implausible, then, not just by the standards of contemporary academic hermeneutics and exegesis, according to which each genre has its own hermeneutical standards, but also by the standards of the authors of the First and Second Testaments themselves.

4.4 The Kingdom of God and the Kingdom of the World

Michał Gierycz has argued that Christianity and especially Roman Catholicism can be what he calls "a hedge or a natural safeguard against fundamentalist tendencies" by bridging the gap between religion and politics not by appeal to eschatology but by appeal to ethics: "By providing an ethical grounding for the political order, particularly by warranting an eschatological distance from political issues, it prevents the kingdom of man being confused with the kingdom of God, thus discarding the fundamentalist logic at its very roots" (Gierycz 2020, 15).

He is onto something here. Jesus Christ emphasizes time and again that his kingdom is not "of this world" (e.g., John 15:19, 18:36). He encourages his followers to give to Caesar what is Caesar's and to God what is God's (Mark 12:17). Such passages have been capitalized upon, for example, in the works of Augustine in the fourth century and Martin Luther in the sixteenth century, who both make a stark distinction between two kingdoms, realms, or regiments: that of God and that of the world—*civitas Dei* and *civitas terrena*, as Augustine called them. The kingdom of God consists of all followers of Christ and does not use any kind of violence. It is ruled by the Word. The kingdom of the world or the secular kingdom consists of earthly kingdoms and governments, and these do inevitably sometimes need to use violence to fight evil. They are ruled by the sword. Therefore, ecclesiastical and civil authorities have different methods and different responsibilities. This doctrine of the two kingdoms also found its way into the theologies of other strands of Christianity, such as Calvinism—via the theologies of Andrew Melville and Francis Turretin—and Anabaptism. In fact, in Roman Catholicism as well, there is acute awareness that Christ was not seeking to overturn the political order and surely was not violent. As Pope Benedict XVI (2007) writes:

> Christianity did not bring a message of social revolution like that of the ill-fated Spartacus, whose struggle led to so much bloodshed. Jesus was not Spartacus, he was not engaged in a fight for political liberation like Barabbas or Bar-Kochba. Jesus, who himself died on the Cross, brought something totally different: an encounter with the Lord of all lords, an encounter with the living God and thus an encounter with a hope stronger than the sufferings of slavery, a hope which therefore transformed life and the world from within.

Any attempt to establish God's kingdom on earth by way of violence goes directly against the doctrine of the two kingdoms. An example of this in Luther's own lifetime was the Münster rebellion in 1534–5, in which extreme and fanaticist Anabaptists with a strongly millenarian apocalyptic vision established a communal sectarian government in Münster, practiced polygamy, and announced that this city would be the New Jerusalem. It ended in a bloody siege of the city and the capture, torture, and death of its radical Anabaptist occupants. The entire rebellion was strongly condemned by Luther. The lack of separation between church and state power can lead to the immanentization of salvation in both religious and secular fundamentalism and fanaticism. The doctrine of the two kingdoms provides resilience capital because it prohibits identifying the two. Now, we already saw that fundamentalism need not employ violence, but where it does, the doctrine of the two kingdoms may provide capital for resilience.[74]

4.5 Apostolic Succession, Hierarchy, and Authority

Other elements of monotheistic capital providing resilience lie at the intersection of belief and practice: they are ideas about apostolic succession and, consequently, church hierarchy and church authority. These ideas are strongly present in the Roman Catholic Church and Eastern Orthodox churches. Pivotal here is the magisterium, the teaching authority of the Roman Catholic Church, vested in the pope and the bishops. Traditionally, Christian churches have held that the Holy Spirit would preserve them from errors in their essential doctrines. This applies in particular to ecumenical church councils, especially the first seven, held between 325 and 787. In 1870, the Roman Catholic Church promulgated that this infallibility is vested in the pope when he speaks ex cathedra on morals or doctrine. Contrast this with Christian fundamentalists: they usually consist of groups and individuals who avoid denominational hierarchy. Their leader is the sole person in charge.[75]

Hierarchy and institutional authority provide resilience toward fundamentalism, because individuals or groups of religious believers cannot all by themselves come to a particular interpretation of scripture that they think is right; they always have to defer to church authority to embrace a specific understanding of a Bible passage. Not only that, but interpretations of Bible passages will also to some extent have to be consonant with the exegetical tradition of the

---

[74] Is there also a distinction between *regnum* and *sacerdotium* in Islam? This is a contested issue. Appleby (1998, 284) claims that "Muslims are unique among the major monotheist traditions because they have never formally accepted and institutionalized a distinction between religion and the state, or between the 'public' and 'private' realms of society." Others, however, disagree (e.g., Pohl 2014, 227).

[75] As noted by Deal and Bartoszuk (2014, 267).

church. Thus, literal-historical interpretations cannot be ruled as the only correct ones, since the majority position in church history is allegorical. From a church-historical perspective, the literal-historical interpretation is primarily a modern response, paradoxically, to modern liberal readings.

Yet this structure of hierarchy and epistemic authority clearly does not guarantee that fundamentalism cannot creep in. This very structure can also itself introduce fundamentalist, fanaticist, or extremist thought and practice into a church if the people in power and with epistemic authority succumb to fundamentalism. Although the church's relation to tradition and the history of interpretation will still render this difficult, it is evidently not impossible—witness, for instance, the radicalization and disastrous influence in the Russian Orthodox Church of Patriarch Kirill, who religiously justified the genocidal war against Ukraine, demonized the entire West, and vilified homosexuals (and LGBTQI+ more generally).

Again, then, we see resilience potential in monotheistic religions, potential that can be valuable in resisting fundamentalism but cannot prevent it completely. This particular piece of resilience capital has to do with doctrine but at least as much with practice, for it concerns not merely what a religious community believes but also how it is organized.

4.6 The Nature of Faith

Another resource within monotheistic religions for resilience toward fundamentalism is the nature of faith. Fundamentalisms often conceptualize faith as a matter of holding the right set of beliefs (orthodoxy) and being certain or being convinced of these beliefs, meaning that doubt and skepticism are the enemies of faith. But recent work in analytic theology and the philosophy of religion stresses that this is a mistake and that it conflicts with how faith has normally been conceptualized in the holy scriptures and in tradition. In fact, much of it argues that faith does not even require propositional belief. Faith in God can come in various shapes and sizes and with numerous propositional attitudes, such as trust, commitment, allegiance, and hope.[76] Belief is not required, let alone certainty. Doubt and questioning are to be welcomed as part and parcel of most people's faith.

Take Daniel Howard-Snyder's account of what he calls "global faith." Here is how he understands this notion:

---

[76] For a recent overview of work on the nature of faith, see Bishop and McKaughan (2022). Leading figures in this debate are John Bishop, Daniel Howard-Snyder, Jonathan Kvanvig, Daniel McKaughan, and Meghan Page.

> For you to be *a person of some particular faith F* is for there to be some
> worldview, grand narrative, ideal, person, etc. such that you have a positive
> cognitive attitude toward F, you have a positive conative orientation toward F,
> you unify important aspects of your life through that attitude and orientation,
> you are disposed to live in light of that attitude, orientation, and unification,
> and you are resilient in the face of challenges to living in that way. (Howard-
> Snyder 2017, 57)

He argues that this conceptualization squares well with the evangelist Mark's
understanding of faith (see Howard-Snyder 2017, 56–8). If he is right, then being
a person of Christian faith requires neither belief nor certainty. Being a person of
faith, whether that be Christian, Islamic, Buddhist, or secular, is a matter of
having a positive attitude toward the content of that religion, being disposed to
live in light of it, and being resilient to challenges to it. In fact, one can thus be
a person of *great* faith without any belief or certainty and while open-mindedly
listening to and conversing with those who hold different worldviews.

This conception of faith is even more important in Judaism, in which doubting
particular interpretations of texts and questioning God are common religious
practices. In fact, Chief Rabbi Jonathan Sacks goes so far as to say that "Judaism
is the rarest of phenomena: a faith based on asking questions, sometimes deep and
difficult ones that seem to shake the very foundations of faith itself" (Sacks 2022).

Let me stress that these are not conceptions of faith later developed to cast
certain texts in a particular mold: these ideas are already present in Christianity
and Judaism's holy scriptures. Take Abraham, for instance, the so-called father of
faith (Romans 4:11–12). Although he is considered the exemplar of faith, his life
was full of doubt and uncertainty, and at various moments he did not rely at all on
God's promises (Genesis 17–21). What made him the father of faith was that in
the end, he trusted God and obeyed him, responding to the call to leave his tribe
and follow God.[77] Another example is Job. Job continually questions God and
even accuses him at certain points of the suffering he has to undergo, while his
friends Eliphaz, Bildad, and Zophar deduce that Job must have sinned. But when
God finally replies, he says that Job's friends have not spoken the truth about him,
whereas Job has (Job 42:7). Finally, Christ himself, as the ultimate exemplar of
faith, had existential doubts in the garden of Gethsemane, begging God to seek
another solution (Mark 14), and at Golgotha he screamed, "My God, my God,
why have you forsaken me?" (Mark 15:34). Yet, at each moment he obeyed God,
despite his doubts. As Daniel Howard-Snyder and Daniel McKaughan (2022,
232) rightly point out: "Exemplars of faith in God continue to rely on God despite
a variety of struggles in doing so, even belief-cancelling doubt."

---

[77] This point is made by Howard-Snyder and McKaughan (2022, 229–30).

4.7 Greater and Lesser Jihad

So far, as announced, we have mostly covered the resources for resilience toward fundamentalism in Christianity and Judaism. Let me also give an example from Islam, though. It is quite common in Islam and Islamic theology to distinguish between the greater jihad and the lesser jihad. The lesser jihad can be divided into the jihad of the pen or tongue—for instance, a public debate—and the jihad of the sword. The greater jihad, which is the more important jihad, is the struggle against one's own wrong impulses and desires, such as wrong sexual impulses, arrogance, and greed. These are all to be brought in conformity with Allah's will.

There is, in fact, a Hadith that tells how the prophet Muhammad upon his return from the battle of Tabuk in 630 said: "We returned from a minor jihad to a greater jihad," which is "the greater jihad of striving against the capricious desires of the self." Admittedly, some have doubted the authenticity of this Hadith (saying it is not *sahih*), but even they confirmed that its meaning is correct, also because there are similar Hadith with the same meaning.[78]

Moreover, research shows most contemporary Muslims embrace the idea that the inner (greater) jihad has primacy over the external (lesser) jihad (see Bonner 2006; see also Abou El Fadl 2002, 37). This distinction, then, may be fruitfully employed in building resilience against fundamentalism, particularly its relatively rare violent manifestations.

4.8 Conclusion

We can conclude that monotheisms—at least Christianity, Judaism, and Islam—provide several resources for resilience toward fundamentalism. We considered and found resilience potential in the Jewish and Christian anthropological-theological notion that humans are created in the image of God, the hermeneutics employed in the holy scriptures of Abrahamic religions, the doctrine of the two kingdoms, the concept and practice of apostolic succession, hierarchy, and authority, the nature of faith as not requiring certainty and possibly not even belief, and the distinction between and relative weight of the greater and lesser jihad in Islam.

We have considered only a few of the many options here. How all this translates, if at all, to public policy is a separate and difficult issue. There are at least two problems in building any bridge between the beliefs and practices of monotheistic religions and political counterfundamentalism strategies. The first one is that, arguably, religion is an end in itself, not an instrument toward some goal,[79] even if that is an admirable goal, such as countering fundamentalism where it is

---

[78] See the fatwas at www.askimam.org/public/question_detail/18385.

[79] This has been argued in several contributions in Van der Borght (2006), particularly in that by Abraham van de Beek.

epistemically or morally harmful. It is not clear, then, that religion can properly be used as a political tool to resist or mitigate the consequences of fundamentalism. That may well conflict with the very nature of religion. Second, in secular Western societies, where many of the readers presumably live, there is a separation between church and state, so that the government should not interfere in the lives of religious communities, and churches or other religious institutions should not meddle in political affairs. In France, there is even *laïcité*, which forbids any public expression of religion, especially in governmental buildings and such institutions as courts of justice and universities. Religion is thought to be strictly private.[80] Moreover, in some cases deradicalization processes go hand in hand with conversion, often from one religion to another; this is clearly something a secular state will not want to be involved with at all.[81]

Yet the religious resilience capital is important even in Western secular countries. On the one hand, it matters to those religious groups themselves. If what I have argued is right, then it is important to continually *teach* religious believers about core ideas, doctrine, concepts, and practices within their religion that build resilience toward fundamentalism. If one worries that this would fail to do justice to the very nature of religion, one can teach these things for the sake of religious knowledge itself—while fully aware that it may well have this side effect. On the other hand, all this matters for the public debate on religion and fundamentalism. The way to counter fundamentalism and related movements is not to publicly denounce religion or monotheism or Islam in particular, as is not uncommon in the West. In the public realm, we should clearly distinguish mainstream religions from their extreme subgroups and acknowledge that fundamentalist subgroups fail to do justice to core tenets of those religions, rather than, say, embodying the allegedly "true spirit of Islam" or some such uninformed thing.

Epilogue

It is time to draw this Element to a close. I argued that fundamentalism is a social movement that arose in the early twentieth century, is both modern and anti-modern, and embraces a cosmically dualistic story as well as a historical narrative in terms of paradise, fall, and redemption. We saw that the notion of fundamentalism is best understood as a family resemblance concept with core cases that exemplify all stereotypical properties, such as early twentieth-century

---

[80] In other countries, things are different, of course. Saudi Arabia, for instance, is well known for its religious counterterrorism policies, such as bringing in the expertise and authority of imams to deradicalize terrorists and other violent extremists (see Boucek 2008).

[81] For the study of an example of the latter in the context of the Levant, in this case the conversion of former violent extremists from extremist Islam to Christianity, see Gustafson (2020, 2023).

Christian evangelical biblical literalism and contemporary Salafi jihadism, and boundary cases that display only some of them, such as Hindu ethnonationalism and radical market capitalism.

We have seen that fundamentalism is a force to be reckoned with in the largest monotheistic religions—Christianity, Islam, and Judaism—no matter how hard it is to attach any exact numbers to this claim. Yet something similar could be argued for *any* major religion and worldview. We saw that fundamentalism permeated contemporary Hinduism, which is largely polytheistic, and that market thinking taken to its extreme can rightly be qualified as a variety of fundamentalism. I submit that mutatis mutandis this also holds for, say, nationalist Sinhala Buddhists—we have seen violent eruptions of Buddhist fundamentalism over the last few years in countries such as Myanmar and Sri Lanka. In secular worldviews, such as atheism and agnosticism, we find not only market fundamentalism but also scientism, right-wing extremism, ecofundamentalism, left-wing radicalism (such as that of the Rote Armee Fraktion), and much more. All these movements can rightly be considered paradigm or boundary cases of fundamentalism. The idea that there is a causal connection between monotheism and fundamentalism whereas there is no such connection between other worldviews and fundamentalism, then, is simply not substantiated by the empirical data.

Something similar holds for the content of monotheistic religions, more specifically, their beliefs and practices. We had to be selective, but much of what is sometimes taken to lead to fundamentalism in a monotheistic religion, such as its belief in only one God, its belief in absolute truth, its soteriological exclusivism, or its doctrine of scripture as infallible, is as such not at all conducive to fundamentalism. Of course, these things have been *used* to motivate and justify fundamentalism—specific texts, treated in isolation, probably more so than doctrines, dogmas, rituals, or practices. Upon closer inspection, though, we saw that much in these monotheistic religions steers away from fundamentalism and can actually provide resilience against it.

All this should not make us assume, out of a secular bias or otherwise, that monotheisms' potential for fundamentalism and their resources for resilience toward fundamentalism are the same across different religions. As worldviews differ in what they say and in what practices they come with, they may well differ in the extent to which they can provide resilience toward fundamentalism. How much potential for fundamentalism each of them has is to be determined only on thorough empirical and theological scrutiny, not a priori out of the misguided idea that fairness requires us to end up with the same assessment for all religions.

Such follow-up inquiry would lead us far into theological debates and issues. For example, how does each of these monotheistic religions and the various denominations within them relate to the political realm? As we saw, some scholars have asserted Islam is inherently political, whereas others have denied this. Which concepts of God exist within the branches of monotheistic religions, and how does each of them relate to fundamentalism? Does it matter, for instance, how authoritative God is thought to be, and how much room there is for questioning God? Are there crucial differences between the lives and ethics of such founding figures as Moses, Jesus Christ, and Muhammad, and to what extent are they thought to be exemplary? These are sensitive issues that deserve meticulous scrutiny and conversation, much more than I can offer here. But it should be clear by now that they deserve further attention.

Let us wrap up. As Peter Huff (2008, 161) points out, "fundamentalism is an enduring and emblematic feature of life in the troubled modern world." I think he is right. But if what I have argued is correct, having a better grip on how fundamentalism relates to monotheism *and* how it does *not* will enable us to better understand, explain, and, where needed, bounce back from fundamentalism or adapt in light of its existence.

References

Abou El Fadl, K. (2002). Peaceful Jihad. In M. Wolfe, ed., *Taking Back Islam: American Muslims Reclaim Their Faith*. Emmaus, PA: Rodale Books, pp. 33–9.

Almond, G. A., Appleby, R. S., and Sivan, E. (2003). *Strong Religion: The Rise of Fundamentalisms around the World*. Chicago, IL: The University of Chicago Press.

Almond, G. A., Sivan, E., and Appleby, R. S. (1995). Fundamentalism: Genus and Species. In M. E. Marty and R. S. Appleby, eds., *Fundamentalisms Comprehended*. Vol. 5 of *The Fundamentalism Project*. Chicago, IL: The University of Chicago Press, pp. 399–424.

Altemeyer, B., and Hunsberger, B. (1992). Authoritarianism, Religious Fundamentalism, Quest and Prejudice. *International Journal for the Psychology of Religion*, **2**, 113–33.

Altemeyer, B., and Hunsberger, B. (2004). A Revised Religious Fundamentalism Scale: The Short and Sweet of It. *International Journal for the Psychology of Religion*, **14(1)**, 47–54.

Alwin, D. F., Felson, J. L., Walker, E. T., and Tufiş, P. A. (2006). Measuring Religious Identities in Surveys. *International Journal of Public Opinion Quarterly*, **70(4)**, 530–64.

Amesbury, R. (2022). Fideism. In E. N. Zalta and U. Nodelman, eds., *The Stanford Encyclopedia of Philosophy*. https://plato.stanford.edu/archives/sum2022/entries/fideism/.

Apicella, C., Norenzayan, A., and Henrich, J. (2020). Beyond WEIRD: A Review of the Last Decade and a Look Ahead to the Global Laboratory of the Future. *Evolution and Human Behavior*, **41(5)**, 319–29.

Appleby, R. S. (1998). Fundamentalism. In R. Wuthnow, ed., *Encyclopedia of Politics and Religion*. New York, NY: Routledge, pp. 280–8.

Appleby, R. S., and Marty, M. E. (2009). Interview: Think Again: Fundamentalism. *Foreign Policy*, November 12. https://foreignpolicy.com/2009/11/12/think-again-fundamentalism/.

Armstrong, K. (2000). *The Battle for God: Fundamentalism in Judaism, Christianity and Islam*. Glasgow: Harper Collins.

Assmann, J. (2005). Monotheism and Its Political Consequences. In B. Giesen and D. Šuber, eds., *Religion and Politics: Cultural Perspectives*. Leiden: Brill, pp. 141–59.

Battaglia, G. (2017). Neo-Hindu Fundamentalism Challenging the Secular and Pluralistic Indian State. *Religions*, **8(10)**, art. no. 216, 1–20.

Beck, U. (2010). *A God of One's Own: Religion's Capacity for Peace and Potential for Violence*. Cambridge: Polity Press.

Beller, J., and Kröger, C. (2021). Religiosity and Perceived Religious Discrimination as Predictors of Support for Suicide Attacks among Muslim Americans. *Peace and Conflict: Journal of Peace Psychology*, **27**(**4**), 554–67.

Bendroth, M. (2014). Fundamentalism and Christianity. In S. A. Wood and D. H. Watt, eds., *Fundamentalism: Perspectives on a Contested History*. Columbia, SC: The University of South Carolina Press, pp. 55–69.

Benedict XVI (2006). Faith, Reason, and the University: Memories and Reflections. Lecture held at the University of Regensburg, Germany, September 12. https://familyofsites.bishopsconference.org.uk/wp-content/uploads/sites/8/2019/07/BXVI-2006-Regensburg-address.pdf.

Benedict XVI (2007). Encyclical Letter *Spe salvi* to the Bishops, Priests and Deacons, Men and Women Religious, and All the Lay Faithfull, on Christian Hope. www.vatican.va/content/benedict-xvi/en/encyclicals/documents/hf_ben-xvi_enc_20071130_spe-salvi.html.

Beyerlein, K. (2004). Specifying the Impact of Conservative Protestantism on Educational Attainment. *Journal for the Scientific Study of Religion*, **43**(**4**), 505–18.

Biale, D., Assaf, D., Brown, B. et al. (2018). *Hasidism: A New History*. Princeton, NJ: Princeton University Press.

Bishop, J., and McKaughan, D. J. (2022). Faith. In E. N. Zalta and U. Nodelman, eds., *The Stanford Encyclopedia of Philosophy*. https://plato.stanford.edu/archives/fall2022/entries/faith/.

Blankinship, K. Y. (2014). Muslim "Fundamentalism," Salafism, Sufism, and Other Trends. In S. A. Wood and D. H. Watt, eds., *Fundamentalism: Perspectives on a Contested History*. Columbia, SC: The University of South Carolina Press, pp. 144–62.

Boldeman, L. (2007). *The Cult of the Market: Economic Fundamentalism and Its Discontents*. Canberra: Australian National University Press.

Bonner, M. (2006). *Jihad in Islamic History: Doctrines and Practice*. Princeton, NJ: Princeton University Press.

Boucek, C. (2008). *Saudi Arabia's "Soft" Counterterrorism Strategy: Prevention, Rehabilitation, and Aftercare*. Washington, DC: Carnegie Endowment for International Peace. https://carnegieendowment.org/files/cp97_boucek_saudi_final.pdf.

Bourget, D., and Chalmers, D. (2023). Philosophers on Philosophy: The 2020 Philpapers Survey. *Philosophers' Imprint*, **23**(**11**), 1–53.

Brandt, M. J., and Van Tongeren, D. R. (2017). People Both High and Low on Religious Fundamentalism Are Prejudiced toward Dissimilar Groups. *Journal of Personality and Social Psychology*, **112(1)**, 76–97.

Bruce, S. (2008). *Fundamentalism*, 2nd ed. Cambridge: Polity Press.

Buijs, G. (2013). Monotheism and Political Violence: Reflections on the Argumentative Sustainability of a Causal Claim. In A. Vanney, ed., *Violence in Civil Society: Monotheism Guilty?* Hildesheim: Georg Olms, pp. 19–36.

Cahan, J. A. (2014). The Jewish Settler Movement and the Concept of Fundamentalism. In S. A. Wood and D. H. Watt, eds., *Fundamentalism: Perspectives on a Contested History*. Columbia, SC: The University of South Carolina Press, pp. 108–24.

Carpenter, J. A. (1997). *Revive Us Again: The Reawakening of American Fundamentalism*. New York, NY: Oxford University Press.

Çelik, Y. (2023). Answering Divine Love: Human Distinctiveness in the Light of Islam and Artificial Superintelligence. *Sophia*. http://doi.org/10.1007/s11841-023-00977-w.

Chakrabarty, B., and Jha, B. K. (2020). *Hindu Nationalism in India: Ideology and Politics*. London: Routledge.

Chisholm, R. M. (1973). *The Problem of the Criterion*. Milwaukee, WI: Marquette University Press.

Choueiri, Y. M. (2010). *Islamic Fundamentalism: The Story of Islamist Movements*. London: Continuum.

Chung, M. G., Kang, H., Dietz, T., Jaimes, P., and Liu, J. (2019). Activating Values for Encouraging Pro-environmental Behavior: The Role of Religious Fundamentalism and Willingness to Sacrifice. *Journal of Environmental Studies and Sciences*, **9**, 371–85.

Clarke, S. (2017). *Competing Fundamentalisms: Violent Extremism in Christianity, Islam, and Hinduism*. Louisville, KY: Westminster John Knox.

Cliteur, P. (2010). *Het monotheïstisch dilemma, of De theologie van het terrorisme*. Amsterdam: De Arbeiderspers.

Cox, H. (2016). *The Market as God*. Cambridge, MA: Harvard University Press.

Crawford, D. D. (2014). The Idea of Militancy in American Fundamentalism. In S. A. Wood and D. H. Watt, eds., *Fundamentalism: Perspectives on a Contested History*. Columbia, SC: The University of South Carolina Press, pp. 36–54.

Dawson, L. L. (2018). Challenging the Curious Erasure of Religion from the Study of Religious Terrorism. *Numen*, **65(2–3)**, 141–64.

Dawson, L. L. (2021a). Bringing Religiosity Back In: Critical Reflection on the Explanation of Western Homegrown Religious Terrorism (Part I). *Perspectives on Terrorism*, **15(1)**, 2–16.

Dawson, L. L. (2021b). Bringing Religiosity Back In: Critical Reflection on the Explanation of Western Homegrown Religious Terrorism (Part II). *Perspectives on Terrorism*, **15(2)**, 1–21.

Deal, J. E., and Bartoszuk, K. (2014). Preliminary Validation of the North American Protestant Fundamentalism Scale. *Journal of Beliefs and Values*, **35(3)**, 265–77.

De Graaf, B. (Forthcoming). *The Radical Redemption Model: Terrorist Beliefs and Narratives*. Extreme Belief and Behavior Series, Vol. 1. New York, NY: Oxford University Press.

De Graaf, B., and Van den Bos, K. (2021). Religious Radicalization: Social Appraisals and Finding Radical Redemption in Extreme Beliefs. *Current Opinion in Psychology*, **40**, 56–60.

Dehlvi, A. H. M. (2006). *Perfection of Faith*. Lahore: Islamic Book Foundation.

Denemark, R. A. (2008). Fundamentalisms as Global Social Movements. *Globalizations*, **5(4)**, 571–82.

Droogers, A. (2005). Syncretism and Fundamentalism: A Comparison. *Social Compass*, **52(4)**, 463–71.

Ecklund, E. H., and Johnson, D. R. (2021). *Varieties of Atheism in Science*. New York, NY: Oxford University Press.

Ellethy, Y. (2023). *Al-walā'w'al-barā'* (Loyalty and Disavowal): Reconstructing a "Creed" in the Muslim Hermeneutics of "Otherness." In B. Reitsma and E. van Nes-Visscher, eds., *Religiously Exclusive, Socially Inclusive?* Amsterdam: Amsterdam University Press, pp. 163–81.

Engels, F. (1880). *Die Entwicklung des Sozialismus von der Utopie zur Wissenschaft*. Hottingen-Zürich: Schweizerischen Genossenschaftdruckerei.

Feldt, L. (2023). Training for Total Devotion: Emotionality and Narrativity in Deuteronomy. *Religion*, **53(1)**, 43–67.

Fernandes, E. (2007). *Holy Warriors: A Journey into the Heart of Indian Fundamentalism*. New Delhi: Penguin Books.

Gierycz, M. (2020). Religion: A Source of Fundamentalism or a Safeguard against It? *Religions*, **11(3)**, art. no. 104, 1–19.

Grigoropoulos, I. N. (2014). Personality Traits as Predictors of Sexual Attitudes in a Sample of Greek University Students. *Psychology and Sexuality*, **5(3)**, 201–9.

Grossman, M. (2021). Resilience to Violent Extremism: A Multisystemic Analysis. In M. Ungar, ed., *Systemic Resilience: Adaptation and Transformation in Contexts of Change*. Oxford: Oxford University Press, pp. 293–317.

Grossman, M., Hadfield, K., Jefferies, P., Gerrand, V., and Ungar, M. (2022). Youth Resilience to Violent Extremism: Development and Validation of the BRAVE Measure. *Terrorism and Political Violence*, **34(3)**, 468–88.

Grube, D.-M. (2023). A Humble Exclusivism? Reconstructing Exclusivism under Justificationist Rather Than Bivalent Parameters. In B. Reitsma and E. van Nes-Visscher, eds., *Religiously Exclusive, Socially Inclusive?* Amsterdam: Amsterdam University Press, pp. 25–41.

Gustafson, S. (2020). Moving toward the Enemy: A Case for Missiological Engagement in Counter/Deradicalization. *Journal for Deradicalization*, **25**, 117–57.

Gustafson, S. (2023). Reshaping the Ultimate Other: Levantine Conversion from Extremist Islam to Christianity through the Lenses of Deradicalization and Missiology. PhD dissertation, Vrije Universiteit Amsterdam.

Hannesson, R. (2014). *Ecofundamentalism: A Critique of Extreme Environmentalism*. Lanham, MD: Lexington.

Harding, S. F. (1991). Representing Fundamentalism: The Problem of the Repugnant Cultural Other. *Social Research*, **58(2)**, 373–93.

Harding, S. F. (2000). *The Book of Jerry Falwell: Fundamentalist Language and Politics*. Princeton, NJ: Princeton University Press.

Harris, J. M. (1994). "Fundamentalism": Objections from a Modern Jewish Historian. In J. S. Hawley, ed., *Fundamentalism and Gender*. New York, NY: Oxford University Press, pp. 137–74.

Heywood, A. (2012). *Political Ideologies: An Introduction*, 5th ed. London: Palgrave Macmillan.

Hick, J. (2004). *An Interpretation of Religion: Human Responses to the Transcendent*, 2nd ed. New Haven, CT: Yale University Press.

Hood, R. W., Hill, P. C., and Williamson, W. P. (2005). *The Psychology of Religious Fundamentalism*. New York, NY: Guilford.

Howard-Snyder, D. (2017). Markan Faith. *International Journal for Philosophy of Religion*, **81**, 31–60.

Howard-Snyder, D., and McKaughan, D. J. (2022). Faith and Resilience. *International Journal for Philosophy of Religion*, **91**, 205–41.

Hudis, P., Vidal, M., Smith, T., Rotta, T., and Prew, P. eds. (2018). *The Oxford Handbook of Karl Marx*. Oxford: Oxford University Press.

Huff, P. A. (2008). *What Are They Saying about Fundamentalisms?* New York, NY: Paulist Press.

Hunsberger, B., Alisat, S., Pancer, S. M., and Pratt, M (1996). Religious Fundamentalism and Religious Doubts: Content, Connections, and Complexity of Thinking. *International Journal for the Psychology of Religion*, **6(3)**, 201–20.

Ibn S̲aalih al-'Uthaymeen, M. (1997). *Explanation of the Three Fundamental Principles of Islaam*. Birmingham: Al-Hidaayah.

Jones, J. W. (2010). Conclusion: A Fundamentalist Mindset? In C. B. Strozier, D. M. Terman, J. W. Jones, and K. A. Boyd, eds., *The Fundamentalist Mindset: Psychological Perspectives on Religion, Violence, and History*. Oxford: Oxford University Press, pp. 216–20.

Kelsey, J. (1995). *Economic Fundamentalism: The New Zealand Experiment—A World Model for Structural Adjustment?* London: Pluto Press.

Kirsch, J. (2004). *God against the Gods: The History of the War between Monotheism and Polytheism*. New York, NY: Penguin.

Krüger, J. S. (2006). Religious Fundamentalism: Aspects of a Comparative Framework of Understanding. *Verbum et Ecclesia*, **27**(**3**), 886–908.

Lawrence, B. B. (1989). *Defenders of God: The Fundamentalist Revolt against the Modern Age*. San Francisco, CA: Harper & Row.

Lehmann, J.-P. (2006). The Dangers of Monotheism in the Age of Globalization. *The Globalist*, March 30. www.theglobalist.com/dangers-monotheism-age-globalization/.

Leitane, I. (2013). Monotheism. In A. L. C. Runehov and L. Oviedo, eds., *Encyclopedia of Sciences and Religions*. Dordrecht: Springer, pp. 1355–64.

Leon, N. (2014). Ethno-religious Fundamentalism and Theo-ethnocratic Politics in Israel. *Studies in Ethnicity and Nationalism*, **14**(**1**), 20–35.

Liht, J., Conway, L. G., Savage, S., White, W., and O'Neill, K. A. (2011). Religious Fundamentalism: An Empirically Derived Construct and Measurement Scale. *Archive for the Psychology of Religion*, **33**(**3**), 299–323.

Livesey, B. (2005). The Salafist Movement: An Examination of the Ideology That Inspired the Global Jihad and the Emergence of Its Most Dangerous Incarnation. *PBS/Frontline*, January 25. www.pbs.org/wgbh/pages/frontline/shows/front/special/sala.html.

Machasin, M. (2009). Civil Islam as an Alternative to Islamic Fundamentalism. In H. Hadsell and C. Stückelberger, eds., *Overcoming Fundamentalism: Ethical Responses from Five Continents*. Geneva: Globethics, pp. 207–25.

Magid, S. (2014a). "America Is No Different," "America Is Different"—Is There an American Jewish Fundamentalism? Part I. American Habad. In S. A. Wood and D. H. Watt, eds., *Fundamentalism: Perspectives on a Contested History*. Columbia, SC: The University of South Carolina Press, pp. 70–91.

Magid, S. (2014b). "America Is No Different," "America Is Different"—Is There an American Jewish Fundamentalism? Part II. American Satmar. In S. A. Wood and D. H. Watt, eds., *Fundamentalism: Perspectives on a Contested History*. Columbia, SC: The University of South Carolina Press, pp. 92–107.

Maimonides, M. (1981). *Commentary on the Mishnah, Tractate Sanhedrin*, edited by F. Rosner. New York, NY: Sepher-Hermon Press.

Marranci, G. (2009). *Understanding Muslim Identity: Rethinking Fundamentalism*. New York, NY: Palgrave Macmillan.

Marsden, G. (1980). *Fundamentalism and American Culture: The Shaping of Twentieth-Century Evangelicalism, 1870–1925*. New York, NY: Oxford University Press.

Marty, M. E., and Appleby, R. S. (1991). Conclusion: An Interim Report on a Hypothetical Family. In M. E. Marty and R. S. Appleby, eds., *Fundamentalisms Observed*. Vol. 1 of *The Fundamentalism Project*. Chicago, IL: The University of Chicago Press, pp. 813–42.

Marty, M. E., and Appleby, R. S., eds. (1991–5). *The Fundamentalism Project*, 5 vols. Chicago, IL: The University of Chicago Press.

Marx, K. (1859). *Zur Kritik der politische Ökonomie: Erstes Heft*. Berlin: W. Besser.

McIntire, C. (1945). *Twentieth Century Reformation*, 2nd ed. Collingswood, NJ: Christian Beacon Press.

Melchert, C. (2011). God Created Adam in His Image. *Journal of Qur'anic Studies*, **13(1)**, 113–24.

Meral, Z. (2018). *How Violence Shapes Religion: Belief and Conflict in the Middle East and Africa*. Cambridge: Cambridge University Press.

Middleton, J. R. (2005). *The Liberating Image: The* Imago Dei *in Genesis 1*. Grand Rapids, MI: Brazos Press.

Missier, C. A. (2022). Fundamentalism and the Search for Meaning in Digital Media among Gen Y and Gen Z. *Journal for Deradicalization*, **33**, 255–85.

Muluk, H., Sumaktoyo, N. G., and Ruth, D. M. (2013). Jihad as Justification: National Survey Evidence of Belief in Violent Jihad as a Mediating Factor for Sacred Violence among Muslims in Indonesia. *Asian Journal of Social Psychology*, **16**, 101–11.

Nanda, M. (2003). *Prophets Facing Backward: Postmodern Critiques of Science and Hindu Nationalism in India*. New Brunswick, NJ: Rutgers University Press.

Newby, G. D. (2014). Conclusion. In S. A. Wood and D. H. Watt, eds., *Fundamentalism: Perspectives on a Contested History*. Columbia, SC: The University of South Carolina Press, pp. 235–52.

Nussbaum, M. C. (2007). *The Clash Within: Democracy, Religious Violence, and India's Future*. Cambridge, MA: Belknap Press.

Ozzano, L. (2017). Religious Fundamentalism and Democracy. *Politics and Religion*, **3**, 127–53.

Peels, R. (2020). Can God Be Jealous? *The Heythrop Journal*, **61(6)**, 964–78.

Peels, R. (2022). On Defining "Fundamentalism." *Religious Studies*, **59(4)**, 729–47.

Peels, R. (2023a). *Ignorance: A Philosophical Study.* New York, NY: Oxford University Press.

Peels, R. (2023b). Scientism and Fundamentalism: What Science Can Learn from Mainstream Religions. *Interdisciplinary Science Reviews*, **48(2)**, 395–410.

Peels, R. (2023c). What Is It to Explain Extremism? *Terrorism and Political Violence.* http://doi.org/10.1080/09546553.2023.2255902.

Peels, R., ed. (Forthcoming). *Extreme Belief and Behavior Series*, 7 vols. New York, NY: Oxford University Press.

Peels, R., and Kindermann, N. (2022). What Are Fundamentalist Beliefs? *Journal of Political Ideologies.* http://doi.org/10.1080/13569317.2022.2138294.

Pew Research Center (2014). *Religious Landscape Study.* www.pewresearch .org/religion/religious-landscape-study/religious-denomination/nondenomi national-fundamentalist/#beliefs-and-practices.

Pfürtner, S. H. (1997). Religiöser Fundamentalismus. *Südosteuropa Jahrbuch*, **28**, 105–16.

Plantinga, A. (2000a). Pluralism: A Defense of Religious Exclusivism. In P. L. Quinn and K. Meeker, eds., *The Philosophical Challenge of Religious Diversity.* Oxford: Oxford University Press, pp. 171–92.

Plantinga, A. (2000b). *Warranted Christian Belief.* New York, NY: Oxford University Press.

Pohl, F. (2014). Islamic Education and the Limitations of Fundamentalism as an Analytical Category. In S. A. Wood and D. H. Watt, eds., *Fundamentalism: Perspectives on a Contested History.* Columbia, SC: The University of South Carolina Press, pp. 217–34.

Ram-Prasad, C. (2005). Contemporary Political Hinduism. In G. Flood, ed., *The Blackwell Companion to Hinduism.* Oxford: Blackwell, pp. 526–50.

Ravitzsky, A. (1996). *Messianism, Zionism, and Jewish Religious Radicalism.* Chicago, IL: University of Chicago Press.

Razaghi, M., Chavoshian, H., Chanzanagh, H. E., and Rabiei, K. (2020). Religious Fundamentalism, Individuality, and Collective Identity: A Case Study of Two Student Organizations in Iran. *Critical Research on Religion*, **8(1)**, 3–24.

Reitsma, B. (2023). Exclusion versus Inclusion: Searching for Religious Inspiration. In B. Reitsma and E. van Nes-Visscher, eds., *Religiously Exclusive, Socially Inclusive?* Amsterdam: Amsterdam University Press, pp. 9–24.

Rouse, S. V., Haas, H. A., Lammert, B. C., and Eastman, K. D. (2019). Same Book, Different Bookmarks: The Development and Preliminary Validation of the Bible Verse Selection Task as a Measure of Christian Fundamentalism. *Journal of Psychology and Theology*, **47(4)**, 278–95.

Ruthven, M. (2004). *Fundamentalism: The Search for Meaning*. Oxford: Oxford University Press.

Sacks, J. (2002). *The Dignity of Difference: How to Avoid the Clash of Civilizations*. London: Bloomsbury.

Sacks, J. (2022). The Necessity of Asking Questions. *OU Torah*. https://out orah.org/p/861#torah.

Sarot, M. (2011). Christian Fundamentalism as a Reaction to the Enlightenment Illustrated by the Case of Biblical Inerrancy. In B. E. J. H. Becking, ed., *Orthodoxy, Liberalism, and Adaptation*. Leiden: Brill, pp. 249–68.

Schwartz, R. (1997). *The Curse of Cain: The Violent Legacy of Monotheism*. Chicago, IL: University of Chicago Press.

Sherkat, D. E., and Darnell, A. (1999). The Effects of Parents' Fundamentalism on Children's Educational Attainment: Examining Differences by Gender and Children's Fundamentalism. *Journal for the Scientific Study of Religion*, **38**(1), 23–35.

Sloterdijk, P. (2007). *Gottes Eifer: Vom Kampf der drei Monotheismen*. Frankfurt am Main: Verlag der Weltreligionen.

Stark, R. (2001). *One True God: Historical Consequences of Monotheism*. Princeton, NJ: Princeton University Press.

Stark, R. (2003). *For the Glory of God: How Monotheism Led to Reformations, Science, Witch-Hunts, and the End of Slavery*. Princeton, NJ: Princeton University Press.

Stone, J. (2000). Dollar Could Use Less Speculation. *Australian Financial Review*, September 20, 25. https://www.afr.com/policy/dollar-could-use-less-speculation-20000920-k9o65.

Streyffeler, L. L., and McNally, R. J. (1998). Fundamentalists and Liberals: Personality Characteristics of Protestant Christians. *Personality and Individual Differences*, **24**(4), 579–80.

Strozier, C. B., Terman, D. M., Jones, J. W., and Boyd, K. A. eds. (2010). *The Fundamentalist Mindset: Psychological Perspectives on Religion, Violence, and History*. Oxford: Oxford University Press.

Taylor, C. (1989). *Sources of the Self: The Making of the Modern Identity*. Cambridge: Cambridge University Press.

Taylor, C. (1995). Two Theories of Modernity. *The Hastings Center Report*, **25**(2), 24–33.

Tibi, B. (2002). *The Challenge of Fundamentalism: Political Islam and the New World Disorder*, updated ed. Berkeley, CA: University of California Press.

Tibi, B. (2013). *The Shari'a State: Arab Spring and Democratization*. New York, NY: Routledge.

Torrey, R. A., ed. (1917). *The Fundamentals: A Testimony to the Truth*, 4 vols. Los Angeles, LA: The Bible Institute of Los Angeles.

Van der Borght, E. A. J. G., ed. (2006). *Religion without Ulterior Motive*. Studies in Reformed Theology, Vol. 13. Leiden: Brill.

Varisco, D. M. (2007). The Tragedy of a Comic: Fundamentalists Crusading against Fundamentalists. *Contemporary Islam*, **1**, 207–30.

Wagemakers, J. (2020). *The Muslim Brotherhood in Jordan*. Cambridge: Cambridge University Press.

Watt, D. H. (2014). Fundamentalists of the 1920s and 1930s. In S. A. Wood and D. H. Watt, eds., *Fundamentalism: Perspectives on a Contested History*. Columbia, SC: The University of South Carolina Press, pp. 18–35.

West, L. (2016). *Distress in the City: Racism, Fundamentalism and a Democratic Education*. London: Trentham Books.

Williamson, W. P. (2020). Conjectures and Controversy in the Study of Fundamentalism. *Brill Research Perspectives in Religion and Psychology*, **2(3)**, 1–94.

Williamson, W. P., Hood, R. W., Ahmad, A., Sadiq, M., and Hill, P. C. (2010). The Intratextual Fundamentalism Scale: Cross-cultural Application, Validity Evidence, and Relationship with Religious Orientation and the Big Factor Markers. *Mental Health, Religion, and Culture*, **13(7–8)**, 721–47.

Wittgenstein, L. (1953). *Philosophical Investigations*. Oxford: Blackwell.

Wnuk-Lipiński, E. (2004). *Świat międzyepoki: Globalizacja, demokracja, państwo narodowe*. Kraków: Znak.

Wood, S. A. (2011). Rethinking Fundamentalism: Ruhollah Khomeini, Mawlana Mawdudi, and the Fundamentalist Model. *Journal of Cultural and Religious Theory*, **11**, 171–98.

Wood, S. A. (2014). The Concept of Global Fundamentalism: A Short Critique. In S. A. Wood and D. H. Watt, eds., *Fundamentalism: Perspectives on a Contested History*. Columbia, SC: The University of South Carolina Press, pp. 125–43.

Wood, S. A., and Watt, D. H., eds. (2014). *Fundamentalism: Perspectives on a Contested History*. Columbia, SC: The University of South Carolina Press.

Acknowledgments

For helpful thoughts, questions, and suggestions regarding issues covered in this Element, I would like to thank various members of the Extreme Beliefs project: Anne Dijk, Daan Dijk, Scott Gustafson, Linda Hasselbusch, Wilma Kannegieter, Nora Kindermann, Naomi Kloosterboer, Clyde Missier, Allan Novaes, Chris Ranalli, and Ruth Tietjen. In addition, I would like to thank Paul Allen, Michael Bakker, Marcel Barnard, Beatrice de Graaf, Yaser Ellethy, Laura Feldt, Dirk-Martin Grube, Daniel Howard-Snyder, Hans Limbeek, Razi Quadir, Jessica Roitman, Marcel Sarot, Victor van Bijlert, Eveline van Staalduine-Sulman, Theo van Willigenburg, and Bart Wallet for helpful comments on the manuscript or ideas elaborated upon in the Element. In the course of the last few years, my numerous constructive conversations with several inspiring scholars have shaped ideas that found their way into this Element. In particular, I would like to mention Tahir Abbas, Tasniem Anwar, Michael Baurmann, Quassim Cassam, Lorne Dawson, Jeroen de Ridder, Richard English, Hina Haq, Jaron Harambam, John Horgan, Nadia Ismaili, Ayhan Kaya, Sophia Moskalenko, Nikolaj Nottelmann, Elanie Rodermond, Charlie Stoeldraaijers, Jan Willem van Prooijen, and René van Woudenberg. I would like to thank Linda Hasselbusch for helping me locate several quotes and references that were hard to retrieve. I thank the students in my 2023 Religion, Violence, and Fundamentalism class, in particular Nastja Tomat, for helpful questions and comments. I thank the editors of the Religion and Monotheism series, Paul K. Moser and Chad Meister, for their helpful guidance and feedback in setting up and writing this Element, as well as an anonymous reviewer for constructive suggestions. Mathanja Berger did yet another meticulous job in carefully copyediting the manuscript, providing astute comments along the way.

Work on this Element was made possible by my project Extreme Beliefs: The Epistemology and Ethics of Fundamentalism, which has received funding from the European Research Council (ERC) under the European Union's Horizon 2020 research and innovation program (grant agreement no. 851613) and from the Vrije Universiteit Amsterdam, the Netherlands. It was also made possible by a smaller grant from the Foundation Oud-Rustenburg (Baambrugge, the Netherlands) for a project of mine on the nature and character of God in religious traditions.

About the Author

Dr. Rik Peels holds a University Research Chair in Analytic and Interdisciplinary Philosophy of Religion at the Department of Beliefs and Practices (Faculty of Religion and Theology) and the Philosophy Department (Faculty of Humanities) at the Vrije Universiteit Amsterdam in the Netherlands. He is also a Senior Research Associate at the African Centre for Epistemology and Philosophy of Science at the University of Johannesburg in South Africa. His research interests are the ethics of belief, ignorance, scientism, fundamentalism, and extremism. He currently leads the ERC-funded project Extreme Beliefs: The Epistemology and Ethics of Fundamentalism (www.extremebeliefs.com). Among his most recent books are *Ignorance: A Philosophical Study* (Oxford University Press, 2023) and *Life without God: An Outsider's Look at Atheism* (Cambridge University Press, 2023). He is the main editor of the seven-volume Extreme Belief and Behavior Series, which is published by Oxford University Press.

Cambridge Elements ≡

Religion and Monotheism

Paul K. Moser

Loyola University Chicago

Paul K. Moser is Professor of Philosophy at Loyola University Chicago. He is the author of *God in Moral Experience; Paul's Gospel of Divine Self-Sacrifice; The Divine Goodness of Jesus; Divine Guidance; Understanding Religious Experience; The God Relationship; The Elusive God* (winner of national book award from the Jesuit Honor Society); *The Evidence for God; The Severity of God; Knowledge and Evidence* (all Cambridge University Press); and *Philosophy after Objectivity* (Oxford University Press); coauthor of *Theory of Knowledge* (Oxford University Press); editor of *Jesus and Philosophy* (Cambridge University Press) and *The Oxford Handbook of Epistemology* (Oxford University Press); and coeditor of *The Wisdom of the Christian Faith* (Cambridge University Press). He is the coeditor with Chad Meister of the book series *Cambridge Studies in Religion, Philosophy, and Society.*

Chad Meister

Affiliate Scholar, Ansari Institute for Global Engagement with Religion, University of Notre Dame

Chad Meister is Affiliate Scholar at the Ansari Institute for Global Engagement with Religion at the University of Notre Dame. His authored and co-authored books include *Evil: A Guide for the Perplexed* (Bloomsbury Academic, 2nd edition); *Introducing Philosophy of Religion* (Routledge); *Introducing Christian Thought* (Routledge, 2nd edition); and *Contemporary Philosophical Theology* (Routledge). He has edited or co-edited the following: *The Oxford Handbook of Religious Diversity* (Oxford University Press); *Debating Christian Theism* (Oxford University Press); with Paul Moser, *The Cambridge Companion to the Problem of Evil* (Cambridge University Press); and with Charles Taliaferro, *The History of Evil* (Routledge, in six volumes). He is the co-editor with Paul Moser of the book series *Cambridge Studies in Religion, Philosophy, and Society.*

About the Series

This Cambridge Element series publishes original concise volumes on monotheism and its significance. Monotheism has occupied inquirers since the time of the Biblical patriarchs, and it continues to attract interdisciplinary academic work today. Engaging, current, and concise, the Elements benefit teachers, researchers, and advanced students in religious studies, Biblical studies, theology, philosophy of religion, and related fields.

Cambridge Elements ≡

Religion and Monotheism

A full series listing is available at: www.cambridge.org/er&m